TEMPLE REFLECTIONS

Paul F. Schmidt

Hummingbird Press   Albuquerque   1980

Library of Congress Catalog Number: 80-80346

ISBN: 0-912998-04-0 (cloth), 0-912998-05-9 (paper)

First Edition

Design by Gail Baker

for Carl F. Schmidt

Father
Companion
Inspiration
Benefactor

Preface

Almost two decades ago I stumbled onto the writings of D. T. Suzuki, found my way into Chan/Zen Buddhism, and into the intimate relationship of aesthetic, religious and philosophical modes of living. Suzuki's *Zen and Japanese Culture* led me to *haiku* and to Bashō's *Narrow Road to the Deep North.* In Bashō's travel diaries I found the fusion that touched my inner self and confirmed me in a new way.

There is a double meaning in the term reflection that brings together aesthetic images from our awareness of nature and art, contemplative religious experience and meditative insights. Each one of these can interact with the others enhancing the totality. Temples provide one concrete focus for such fusions; nature another. Travel may be an art that journeys among temples and nature, creating patterns of consciousing that constitute reflection. This is my dream.

Earlier versions of this book have benefited from the suggestive comments of many friends and students who have read or heard all or part of it. Among them I am grateful to Matthieu Casalis, Patricia Sanborn Glassheim, Howard McConeghy, Evelyn McConeghy, Jim Hiner and Jerry Tecklin. Dan Odell and Gail Baker improved, step by step, every page along the way.

Also by Paul F. Schmidt

Religious Knowledge (1961)

*Perception and Cosmology
in Whitehead's Philosophy* (1967)

*Rebelling, Loving and Liberation:
A Metaphysics of the Concrete* (1970)

Contents

Journey to Japan

Bashō, the Japanese *haiku* poet, begins his *Narrow Road to the Deep North* with a meditation on the possible death that faces a wanderer, a traveler. Not only physical death but a spiritual transformation that may initiate a whole new being. As I hand the latch key to my friends and depart for a year in Japan, Java, India, Iran, Sicily and Greece, I wonder how I shall return.

We want to visit holy places, past and present, in a long personal meditation on their architecture and art, literature and liberation. It is a long way from Albuquerque to Kyoto; many miles and many places can leave an impression on our consciousing. To leave one's culture with its familiar patterns yields a kind of freedom to explore new cultures, to experiment with new patterns. Why not try to create within the *haiku* form some distillations of impressions?

The *haiku* form within the Japanese poetic diary reaches a perfection in the writings of Matsuo Bashō (1644-1694). My journals are spotted with poetic efforts, images of places where my consciousing felt inspiration. The prospect of Japan, of tracing Bashō's steps, stimulates the sharp lens of *haiku*. Concrete three-line poems of five, seven and five syllables take form in my reflecting. I am aware of how creating within a form gives freedom a structure that avoids chaos, and gives choosing a matrix in which to unfold.

> Japanese journey
> Full of *haiku* blossoming
> Bursting days of joy

As we leave Albuquerque on the first quarter of the fifth moon of 1972, a late spring sandstorm fills the air with dust and sand, eats away the glass of our windshield, blinds our vision, clogs our nostrils, warns us of the dangers we face. All afternoon and the next morning we buffet it.

> Wayfaring westward
> Seeking Buddha's serene smile
> Wind and sand buffet
>
> Fine sand clogs my nose
> As I begin my journey
> What will free the air?

As we travel we often read aloud to each other, adding another dimension to experience. Books that suit such a situation are rare discoveries having a texture of sounds that bear speaking and ideas that yield further conversation. Two evenings ago a friend introduced us to a novel by Pär Lagerkvist, *The Sibyl.* The oracular speaks from many places, not only ancient Delphi in Greece. Who knows which holy places among our visits will shatter our familiar being with paradoxical messages? Who arrives may not depart the same.

Two days across Navajo land, the canyons deepen, the rocks grow into fantastic forms awakening in memory other far-away places and things. We camp on the north rim of Grand Canyon, our focus a vista into Transept Canyon, and hike around its head far out on Widforass Point named for a Swedish painter who loved its perspectives. An explorer of the Canyon and a painter in prose, Major Powell, gave us the names of the great rock formations we gaze at.

> Widforass Point I go
> Viewing Deva and Brahma
> Zoroaster too

We spread our clothes upon a flat ledge overlooking this great cleft in the earth and lunch on thick pancakes flavored with raisins and sweetened with honey, a tasty trail lunch we discovered years ago. Warmed in the sun we stretch out, our hiking legs relax, we caress and love and nap before the long walk back.

Canyons are of many kinds. We move from the Grand to Zion, from top ledges to craning our necks to see up from the floor, from overlook to canyon bottom. Upstream the canyon narrows, the water shuttles from side to side, but sometimes after rain a solid wall of water roars through.

> Barefoot, sore and bruised
> Sky a twisted ribbon above
> Zion canyon narrows

What water can do to the earth — make plants and trees grow but also wash away the soil exposing layers of stone in fantastic colors. Erosion destroys soil and creates rock splendor. Cedar Breaks National Monument and Bryce Canyon are two such gardens of rock, blends of colors and shapes, pink, rose, brown, red, gray, ochre, sandy in subtle combinations reflecting the late afternoon light at the bottom of ravines. Deep drifts of snow contrast with the fresh green of the bristlecone pines.

> Cedar Breaks, Utah
> Spires, fins, pinnacles, pines
> Red, brown, pink, rose, gray

> Iron oxide stains
> Red, sulphur-yellow and white
> Dim sunset white moon

We are tired of official campgrounds in the National Parks — those canvas motel stops with flush toilets and running water. Tonight we find our own sort of place, completely alone on the oxbow bank of a stream lacing a grassy meadow. Watching the swallows all the while, we cook and read, frying eggplant and reading aloud Oliver Statler's *Japanese Inn*. The air is criss-crossed with flashes of iridescent green on the swallows. A delicate sky-blue western bluebird sings from a nearby weedstalk. Camped alone we can forget our clothing, slip out of the sleeping bag to piss, or in the morning shower each other in the warm sunshine.

> Swallows dip swooping
> Curving around this oxbow
> Meandering snake

The next day we drive west across the Great Salt Desert to the Humboldt Range.

West of Humboldt Range
Exquisite snow patch lacework
Full moon, end of May

In the morning we bathe in a clear irrigation ditch carrying snow melt to the meadows, the swift current washing out bead-size gravel pebbles around our feet. Dawn the next day is auspicious, for as I watch the moon set till only a slim white crescent remains, at that precise moment the sun rises blinding my eyes — a perfect elevation to camp at.

Days later, several hundred feet above the cliff-rock of the Oregon coast, I witness a vast undulating plane of blue water, a plane that begins vertically below me and slants upward to the distant horizon. Curving arcs of white foam break and roll in. Off shore half a dozen reef-like rocks barely out of the water cause ovals of white on the blue surface. Standing on the beach I cannot see the sea like this.

Off shore rock pattern
Creates white sea-foam patches
Foaming Zen garden

Backpacking along the Pacific coast of the Olympic Peninsula, we leave from the Hoh River mouth emptying into the sea its blue-gray glacial silt from Mt. Olympus glaciers. Two young women returning give us their tide chart, for dangerous headlands can only be passed at low tide. Each is a coastal barrier gate closed and opened by the positions of moon and sun. As the sun reaches its zenith we reach the first tidal barrier gate — closed, so we stop for lunch, waiting, watching from a high boulder.

Tidal barrier gate
Blocks our passage at noontime
Breakers carve sea caves

Gradually the waves retreat, revealing stepping stones around. Tired of waiting we take off our shoes, roll up our trousers and leap from rock to rock, waves lapping our feet. Hoh Headland next, impassable at any tide. Our trail climbs steeply up the cliff through the tropical rain forest.

Sunlight filtered through
Thousand-needled hemlock branch
Spots before my eyes

We sleep on the beach very close to the cliff yet high tide in the night comes within a yard of our sleeping bag. Starfish, orange and purple, cling to the rocks, groups with fingers entwined, five fingers. How often does nature create with the pentagon? It is not easy to divide a circle thus. Starfish do it to perfection.

> Foggy, misty morn
> Orange and purple starfish cling
> Firm on low-tide rocks

Low tide bares a sandbar leading to a high-tide island. Resting in a sea cave a new vision occurs as I watch a breaker rolling in, rushing away from me in a crescent of white foam. This graceful arc casts itself upon the shore to die.

> Crescent-shaped breakers
> Seen rolling in from behind
> A whole new vision

Driftwood makes of every camper an architect of beach shelters. The shore presents a variegated lumber yard of logs, planks, beams, and sections of logs for chairs. We, too, are unable to resist this passion and erect a frame for our fly, benches and table. We talk of building a whole house inspired by many four-by-four beams strewn along this beach, remains perhaps of the wreck of a lumber barge. Every child builds castles in the sand, scoops out moats, drips wet sand like mortar into turrets while waves beat against the outer bastions. So the child begins to travel in daydreams. Our dreams become real as we leap across this Pacific to Japan in a long ten-hour afternoon flight from one day into the next, crossing the international date line, time lost forever.

> Rainier to Fuji
> East and West Pacific peaks
> Pivots of our trip

By sunset we are lodged in our first *ryokan*, a Japanese inn, our bed spread on the *tatami* mats made of rice straw, green tea served on a low table. Delightfully tired, we slip into fresh kimonos and go to the steaming bath, a communal pool where a dozen can soak till pink as a steamed crab. Nothing else prepares one for sleep so well. The Japanese have made bathing an art as much as the tea ceremony and flower arranging. We have reached Japan, a new land and culture to live in.

Kyoto Temples

On the east wall of the next room hang two ink-brush scrolls of the lunatic Zen monk who gazed too long at the moon and became moon struck. A strange smile plays over his face, a mysterious combination of serenity, silliness and profundity. For some time I have gazed at him and only now begin to sense his enlightenment from lunacy.

What might happen to me as I sit in meditation, *zazen*, each morning from seven till eight in Chotoku-in, one of the Zen Temples making up the complex of temples called Shokoku-ji? *Zazen* begins with the 'ting' 'ting' of a small bell calling me to the meditation room, *zendo*, where are placed square flat firm pillows with a small firm circular pillow on top to sit on. I assume a half-lotus position, flex my neck, bend my back to side and front, letting my spine come to rest in a balanced vertical position. Our teacher enters, we make a small bow, he plays the two gongs and bell, begins to chant a sutra on negating, not-this, not-that, not-A, not-B, etc., etc., ends by clapping wood blocks and lighting an incense stick. A long silence ensues of concentration-on-breathing meditation, broken midway by the bell and wooden clappers. At the end of this hour I carefully uncross and unbend my legs, flexing them slowly, rise and go to breakfast.

Sohaku Ogata, Abbot of Chotoku-in awaits us. He is an old man now, no longer able to walk without help, no longer able to conduct morning *zazen*. His eldest son Yugi, future abbot, does so. But his mind is still bright and humorous. He delights most in telling and commenting on old Zen stories. If the conversation turns to chit-chat he is likely to doze off in his chair. His life is now wholly devoted to translating into English *Ching Tê Ch'uan Têng Lu, The Transmission of the Dharma Lamp* (in Japanese *Keitoku Dento Roku*), a lifelong dream. In August 1972 he is at work on scroll eleven out of thirty scrolls. Ogata-san passed on at the Spring equinox, 1973, a balanced day.

We live in a *tatami* mat room. Each such rice-straw mat is three by six feet by three inches thick. The size of any room is a multiple of *tatami* mats which can be arranged in various geometric patterns, an art as seemingly simple, yet as complex as flower arranging, *kabuki* composition or rock garden design. Great subtlety in utter simplicity is the result, the essence of this Japanese aesthetic. What a joy to slide back any wall of your room and unite into one whole whatever is beyond it. Rice-paper panels slide open walls on gardens, joining outside to inside. Our east and south walls are *fusuma*, paper on both sides of the light wood frame. Each of the four sliding panels making the wall is the size of a *tatami* mat, and has a painting in ink-brush of bamboo or grass. Open, they unite the room beyond. The west wall slides open on to a veranda, one mat in width, a rock and moss garden beyond, each stone placed with great care. A bamboo border sets off a few small palms. Half the north wall is a *tokonoma*, a recessed alcove in which hangs a beautiful calligraphy scroll. On one side are flowers re-arranged every few days, on the left a wood carving. These set on a riser six inches above the mats.

Aesthetic simplicity is further expressed in the room furnishings. These are minimal, hardly noticeable, a floor mattress for a bed that is rolled up and put away in the daytime, a low table, some pillows to sit on. I use the low table as a desk sitting lotus posture before it. These are Buddhist rooms, sparsely furnished, serving multiple purposes. Our temple room is a unity of aesthetic simplicity and diverse uses that brings nature inside and takes you outside. Here is an architecture of the One.

Kyoto has a thousand temples, each with gardens, gardens such as I've never seen, of raked gravel, rocks and moss, ponds and trees. In the vast Daitoku-ji Zen temple-complex we contemplate our first garden of raked gravel and rock at Daisen-in, a sub-temple. You will not find flowers in the southeast garden. Instead, there are two conical piles of fine gravel and a single tree on a perfectly flat surface that has been raked into two-inch contours. The cones and tree seem randomly placed while the contours curve past the cones. In such simplicity the Japanese Zen garden manifests the Tao, the indescribable way. Or the garden shows the contingent as absolute, a chance arrangement that must be.

Another garden consists of three groups of rocks and a shrub-tree, the gravel raked in horizontal lines except for concentric circular patterns around each group of rocks. I feel the contrast of concentricity and horizontality combined with the motion and rest of the eye moving from rock to rock. The garden is a resolution of contradictories, a harmony, thoroughly Zen. We pass several hours easily looking upon such a garden.

Across the city at Honen-in you knock three times with the big wooden mallet on a thick square of wood hung by rope. Soon you hear sandaled feet, and a priest ushers you to the Buddha Hall where Amida Buddha awaits you. The Jodo sect believes that complete salvation can be achieved by one enlightened utterance of his name. Left alone, we see an altar rivaling any Catholic altar. In the center sits a six-foot Buddha, Amida, surrounded by beautifully carved candlesticks, vases of fresh flowers, fruit offerings, carved gold-leafed flowers, painted scrolls. Round and round our eyes travel enchanted by our freedom to inspect each item.

> "Amida Buddha"
> Honen taught people to say
> Simple salvation

In summer, day after day, the sky may drip with rain but that makes a moss garden all the more beautiful, as a thousand jewel drops glisten on a moss bed. How can each garden seem superlative? Is it because the absolute is harmonious in the contingent as the Buddha-nature is in everything?

Many think the perfect garden creation is at Ryoan-ji Temple. Twice I've sat for several hours in contemplation of its three gardens. The famous one is raked gravel in which are placed five groups of rocks, each group encircled by a small moss border. Passing through the entrance room you view it from a veranda along a long side of its rectangular form. You cannot step into this garden but you may sit in contemplation of its arrangement and forms. Iconographical interpretations vary: the rocks might be

mountains or ships or islands; the raked sand the sea. A Zen story
tells us that when you first begin to meditate, mountains are
mountains, later on, mountains are no longer mountains, finally
mountains become just what they are. Just so, this garden. As you
turn the corner to your right at the end of the veranda a second
garden appears. It is constructed of a thick moss bed backed with
slim maple trees whose autumnal colors jewel the moss. Turning
the next corner reveals a small stream flowing over a tiny waterfall
into a still pond surrounded by shrubs and rock. From the silence
of the first garden to the flowing watercourse of the way, we have
three movements in a musical composition. Ryoan-ji gives you the
history of Zen gardens. The first is not alone.

> Gravel, moss or pond
> Dry gray, cool green or goldfish
> Ryoan-ji gardens
>
> Velvet smooth green moss
> Wind tips the maple bow down
> Turquoise butterfly

I find a penetrating aesthetic integration among aspects of
the Japanese garden, Noh play, *haiku*, scroll painting, flower
arranging, tea ceremony and *tatami* floor mats. Each creates with
a very limited medium, each manipulates that medium according
to a restricted set of moves, each move clearly accented; each
confines itself to a precise boundary; each achieves a powerful
simplicity that contains a harmony of contrasts; each moulds the
contingent into an expression of the absolute. As I explore each of
these arts I sense striking parallels. Does the farmer design the
contours of his rice paddies according to the same aesthetic ideal?

> Tea ceremony
> Threefold flower arrangement
> *Tatami* texture

Temple floors and Japanese homes are covered with *tatami*
mats of rice straw, soft yet firm, nothing more comfortable to walk
on, kneel on, sit on. Room sizes progress in regular square and
rectangular sizes beginning with a two-mat guard room of six by
six, then six by nine, the four and a half-mat tea room of nine by
nine, then nine by twelve, twelve by twelve, twelve by fifteen,
fifteen by fifteen and so on, the larger the room the more creative

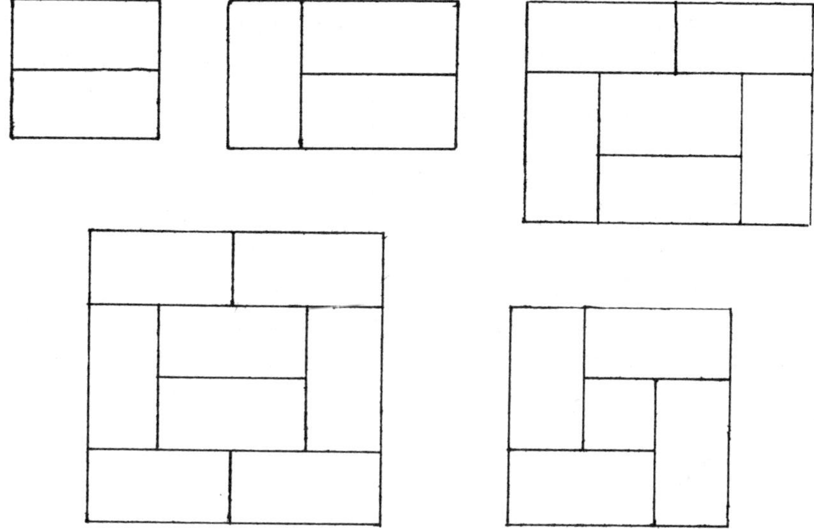

possibilities for arranging mat patterns. The four and a half-mat tea room and the eight-mat chamber are classic forms like the *haiku* and *waka*. Plato in the *Timaeus* displayed a similar geometrical aesthetic in the ultimate forms of the elements using several right triangles, the square and the pentagon. Set a child to arranging mats and you may have an architect.

At five in the morning early dawn light and the songs of birds wake me. My eyes open on the moon-struck monk scrolls. I like to lie still in the glory of the new day. Half an hour later bells ring for *zazen* from the neighboring temple. After three gongs someone begins to beat a rhythm on a tight-skinned drum, shifting to the wooden drum and bass drum. Hardly noticed, the sutra chant begins, swells, replaces the drumming till the tinkle of the tiny bell signals the beginning of silent meditation.

> Terse Buddhist drum beats
> Many voices sutra chanting
> Rain begins and ends

In Koryu-ji Temple you will see the most graceful Buddha in Japan, a carving in wood of Miroku Bosotsu. So many Buddha figures are lifeless, others merely representative, but this one shows the most subtle curves, delicate proportions and soft texture. Were it not a Buddha you would agree it is a beautiful woman whose hands, fingers, back and torso are deftly turned.

> Most graceful Buddha
> Soft Miroku Bosotsu
> Bewitching vision

Tucked in a rice-terraced valley northwest of Kyoto lies Ohara, a quiet farming village with two enchanting temples: Sanzen-in and Jakko-in. In the garden of Sanzen-in you will be blessed on your travels by a sculptured Jizo, protector of children and travelers, of whom there are more images than all other Buddhas combined. Every cemetery, every road, every trail has many Jizos to give help, many dressed in a red cloth bib or apron, unfortunately often covering fine stone carving. Even the butterfly feels safe perched on his head.

> Dancing butterfly
> Alights to rest on Jizo
> His red bib missing!

My friend Jerry Tecklin arrives from Antai-ji, a Soto Zen temple where he has shared their religious life. We talk about their heavy emphasis on *zazen*, making it almost the exclusive vehicle for enlightenment in Zen. To do so, I think, distorts the person and the Tao because it singles out one approach, *zazen*, as the approach. To select one route exclusively divides the undivided. To divide the One misses the Tao. Equally questionable is the immense strain, physical and psychological, of a *sesshin*, intensive *zazen*, a strain that desires relaxation afterwards in sakē or cigarettes. To strain is to force, to compel, to achieve through domination. Thus the self may be forced into a constrained enlightenment but I wonder if such enlightenment is genuine and lasting. When and if it happens is beyond the realm of force; it is effortless, self-sufficient. Strain is not the way. The way is effortless, a joyous balance of aspects of the world-divided-one, a harmony that may reach beyond or create the One. Insofar as any sect selects some aspect to emphasize to the exclusion of others, it cannot be a way to the One. The ascetic and aesthetic blend into unity.

A steady light rain falling on the moss garden. I have slid back the rice-paper screens of my room so I am in the garden but not in the rain. This is the perfection of the Japanese home. You are in nature, the garden enters your room, there is no dividing line, no wall of separation. You participate in the raining, your existing is a rainy living. Your alienation from nature is overcome. I sit reading on the *tatami*, the rain gently falling next to me. I can reach out and touch it. The softest breeze I feel on my skin yet I am never cold. The rocks glisten in the wet light. Why not build a home like this?

On top of Mount Hiei lived the warrior-monks of Enryaku-ji Temple who sometimes swept down on Kyoto to intercede in political affairs, attacking other monasteries to insure the dominance of their sect. I find this history despicable, not Buddhist in any sense. May they all inherit the bad karma of their deeds. Midway between the eastern and western precincts, where tourists rarely walk, I came upon the unusual moss and rock garden of Jodo-in where the moss undulates over small mounds, giving motion to the still garden. New monks here practice an austerity called "sweeping hell," six hours of sweeping each day for three months. Even during a late afternoon service, I see in back of the temple a monk sweeping Saicho's tomb built by the priest Ennin in 854.

> Sweeping life away
> He seeks his liberation
> Leaves forever fall

To seek the aesthetic, avoid the spectacular, leave the big-name places to the tourists, let the tour buses park at Tofuku-ji while you walk to the sub-temple of Taiko-in on the west side. Here you will find intimate harmony undisturbed, from the ceiling lamp in the *zendo* to the mountain profile garden. Look at the screen of painted birds, the small statue of Hyakusai by Komachi, and the tea room built in 1599 by the eleventh abbot, Ankokuju Ekei. The seemingly haphazard tea room, its ceiling of three levels in three different materials, the odd-shaped windows in odd places, one of its four and a half mats replaced by a wooden floor, and a single off-center vertical thin column, illustrates the aesthetic of incongruity. The east garden of rocks and moss beyond the pond mirrors the silhouette of mountain ridges to the east.

> Raindrops on stone bridge
> White butterfly on green moss
> Careless I wander

There is a deep affinity between pigeons and temples whose roof shapes and eaves provide ideal places to roost. Many temples have constructed elaborate chicken-wire screens to keep the faithful pigeons from meditating near Buddha. Where such screens are not in place, beware a pigeon greeting. Perhaps they also deter the uninterested tourist.

> Buddhas sit and sit
> While tourists gawk and gawk
> Pigeons shit and shit

I do not believe in reincarnation as a literal metaphysical event but I do think it guides your reflection to a consideration of the moral value of your actions when combined with the concept of Karma and, further, it lets you connect your present life to the lives of others for whom you feel deep sympathy and identity. Reading Thoreau's *Journal* and his biographies has always aroused in me a sense of identity that I cannot explain. A similar feeling came to me in the Kyoto Museum when I saw some scroll paintings of Bodhidharma, an Indian monk who brought Buddhism to China. I sat and stared at him for more than an hour. Somewhere back before Thoreau I felt an identity with Bodhidharma. I couldn't help noticing his big nose, his bulging hanging eyelids resting on his upper eyelashes, the wrinkles spreading into his cheeks from the corners of his eyes, his hairy chest in his faded red robe.

> Faded torn red robe
> Eyelids bulging over eyes
> Huge nose and ear rings
> Smile wrinkles on his cheeks
> Bodhidharma stares at me

Katsura Garden, an Emperor's villa, turns the Japanese garden into an extravaganza. Leave its artificial and contrived complexity to those who seek the footsteps of power. Walk through the back streets to Saiho-ji, the moss garden temple, for shadows and sunlight filtered through trees onto undulating moss and carp-rippled pond. Follow the path in both directions because

each corner holds its revealing vision. At the tiny outlet from the
pond, running clear from cloudy water, ponder why

> No carp swimming out
> From Saiho-ji garden pond
> No trout swimming in

You may hear a strange periodic thud along the path. Look
around and you will see a piece of bamboo teetering on a hinged
stick, filling with water from a tiny riverlet until the increased
weight tips it down, pouring out the water and teetering back with
a thud when the end strikes the ground. This thud may awaken
you. I stood entranced, filling with water, teetering, making my
thud.

> Bamboo tube teeters
> When water slowly fills it
> Falling back it thuds

Suppose you met a tiger who never took his eyes off you! At
Sangen-in in Daitoku-ji there is such a tiger painted on the wall
screen. You can begin at one side of the room constantly watching
the tiger's eyes, walk across to the opposite side; his eyes follow
your every step and his head seems to turn as you move. A
haunting painting, an unceasing unity of you and tiger.

> A tiger whose eyes
> Follow you from side to side
> Fixed yet turning head

At Obai-in in Daitoku-ji the gravel in the garden conveys a
vivid sense of the undulating motion of the sea. The gravel has
been raked in a flattened sine curve. As I sit in contemplation the
gravel surface begins to move, gentle swells about the rocks. Soon
I am the waves, rhythmic diastole of the pulse of this garden. I
begin to breathe in unison with it. And what are the temple
buildings now but ships that sail on land, the curved-up corners of
their tile roofs bows that sail in four directions. This upward curve
creates a feeling of lightness, buoyancy; floating arks that may
ferry you across.

> Soft gentle sea waves
> From undulating gravel
> Temples sailing free

Pilgrimage around Honshu

Curving around the shores of Lake Biwa the electric train cuts through low sharp hills dense with green trees, every tiny valley leveled in descending terraces of rice paddies, countryside described by Bashō in his *Essay on the Vision-Inhabited House.* We shall retrace in reverse direction some portions of Bashō's *The Narrow Road to the Deep North.* Mid-afternoon we change trains in Fukui and ascend a valley to Eihei-ji Temple, founded by the famous Zen monk Dōgen (1200-1254). Perched on three levels on a hillside, shaded by giant cryptomeria, nowadays Eihei-ji is unfortunately a major tourist attraction as well as an important pilgrimage place.

> Dōgen taught Zazen
> Left China empty handed
> Be empty, sit still

We wondered where to lodge. Walked upstream to scout a place for our sleeping bags. Returned to town for our packs and stumbled on the Japan Youth Hostel. Not so young yet they let us in and we enjoyed lodging with the students. Supper was delicious — soup, rice, breaded pork, hard-boiled egg, shredded cabbage, tomato, smoked fish, tempura fish, and green tea. In the *ofuro*, Japanese group bath, I watch and learn how to dump water from a small bucket over myself, soap thoroughly and rinse off before entering the hot steaming bath for six. At breakfast we learn how to break a raw egg into a bowl, add soy sauce, mix and pour over hot rice, as common a dish as bacon and eggs at home, refreshing and filling. A bowl of miso soup made from dried fish and various flavored bean pastes completes the traditional Japanese breakfast, quite unvarying during our month of pilgrimage. We wash our own dishes, sweep out the room and hall and so reduce the cost of lodging for traveling students.

Visualize a letter 'H' on a hillside with a building across the bottom and top, and you have the ground plan of Eihei-ji. Each horizontal building stands on a terrace above the lower one. Water has been channeled into the temple grounds and cascades down, a pleasing sound, and you are cool beneath the shade of tall cryptomeria. On the ceiling of the reception hall are hundreds of circular paintings, each a gem to behold. We lie on our backs looking intently at different sections of the ceiling, flowers, birds, trees in blossom, animals; clearly a room in which to do *zazen* lying down, Amida's paradise on the ceiling.

While Bashō traveled southward returning from the north, we go northward reaching Yoneyama, literally rice mountain, where a headland juts out into the sea, site of an old barrier gate. We spend the night in a *minshuku*, traveler's inn, and swim at sunset and sunrise in the Sea of Japan. In the morning we climb to the site of the old barrier gate marked by an inscription on a large stone. What was the weather and view when Bashō presented his identification for scrutiny in the seventeenth century? Small towns are a good place to stay, easy to find your way around, easier to glimpse something of the life of the people. Our Inn is owned and managed by a young man, eighth in a line of successive generations rebuilding portions of the Inn as they wear out.

> Yoneyama gate
> Entrance to unknown shrines
> Beckons us northward

We wonder where we will stay the next night as our second-class train stops at each small station. We prefer the second-class train because it goes slow enough for us to see the country and the people. On the bullet express, 100 mph, from Tokyo to Kyoto, it was impossible to see life in the village streets, too fast for the eye. Our companion Gene Sager is able to speak Japanese, and his conversation with a student couple on the train led to an invitation to spend the night at their home on a farm in the village of Nakajo outside of Niigata.

Hospitality
Simple warmth and gracefulness
Summer evening meal
Blending tastes unknown to us
Compassionate farming hosts

Our bed lay on the floor under a vast mosquito net eight by eight by five high suspended from hooks in the high wall of the room, a tent free of *ka* (mosquitoes). Pillows are shaped like cylinders, very firm, four inches in diameter. You are supposed to sleep in a *yukata*, a bathrobe with great square sleeves, one *yukata* fitted inside another, the outer one padded like a heavy quilt, the inner one soft cotton. Strange are the ways people have learned to sleep; each seems restful to those accustomed to it. I enjoy the changes and generally sleep well, yet the pillow was as hard as I ever had.

Up at six to accompany the farmer into his gardens and barns. He washes his hands and face in the swift clean irrigation ditch. We do the same. All sorts of vegetables supply their needs: potatoes are spread drying on the barn floor, onions are hung in bunches, fruits are drying in the sun. Two thick-walled rice storage buildings dominate the farmyard. Good health and self-sufficiency is the impression I have.

On a branch line of the railroad that follows the coast we make a pilgrimage to the town of Izumozaki, home of the priest-poet Ryokan (1758-1831). A fine small museum displays some of his manuscripts and beautiful calligraphy plus some scroll paintings depicting his life, his love of children, his dancing on the beach in sheer joy, his simplicity. Below the museum is a little park where Bashō stopped to rest. Let Ryokan sing:

Water I will draw,
Firewood I will cut,
Vegetables I will pick
In the space before
Autumn's showers fall.

The wind is gentle
The moon is bright
Come then, together
We'll dance the night out
As a token of old age.

At the foot of Mt. Haguro we put up in a Shugendo Temple that functions as an inn for pilgrims, providing a service in the evening before their climb next morning. To climb Mt. Haguro, Mt. Gassan and Mt. Yudono is a lifetime sacred act — a tradition Bashō honored. The Shugendo sect is a strange combination of Buddhist, Shinto and Folk beliefs in which special powers acquired through ascetic practices in the mountains belong to the *yamabushi*, mountain men. I, too, often feel the power, the joy, the ecstacy, when rambling alone in the mountains, bathing in icy streams, perched on a rocky ledge.

The sacred path begins when you pass beneath a large *tori*, the distinctive Shinto gate, descend the first flight of old uneven stone steps, and cross the stone bridge to the first group of Shinto-like shrines. I am now deep in a forest of ancient cryptomeria trees (cedars) like our California redwoods. I am thrust heavenward by these awesome trees. Looking through a deep ravine in the trees I see a tall pagoda mounting skyward with the cedars, fit company for tall trees.

> Rigid pagoda
> Growing cedars sweep past it
> Time topples desire

Disappearing in the twilight of the trees, endless stone steps ascend the mountain, worn uneven, closely flanked by giant trees, living *tori*, 1000 years old, hardly space for another tree between them.

> Endless stone steps rise
> Entice you into twilight
> Meditative lure
>
> Cryptomeria
> Line the path like *tori* gates
> Climbing Haguro

In each holy place I wondered why small pebbles rested on any ledge or flat space of *tori*, Jizo, or stone lantern. How do they get there, sometimes very high up? I learned that if you deftly throw one and it stays on the ledge, good luck is yours. I think of the stone cairn marking Thoreau's cabin and realize that placing or throwing a stone memorializes your pilgrimage, joins your spirit, your life, to another spirit. Creative power flows from such linkage.

Midway up Haguro a side path leads to a clearing where the foundation stones mark the site of an ancient inn where Bashō stayed. The garden ponds are filled with fallen leaves. The stone slab bridge to the islet and stepping stones to another islet guide all footsteps, his and mine, in the exact same steps. He may have sat on the same stone gazing across the pond at the inn, reflecting on his journey.

> Tracing Bashō's steps
> To each islet in the pond
> In reflection cast

In a corner of the clearing stands an old chestnut tree. For how many years did its shade comfort weary pilgrims?

> Foundation stones stand
> Where once an inn graced the land
> Hot chestnuts served man

Mt. Gassan towers over Mt. Haguro. It is an all-day climb on a trail so well worn by pilgrims that in places it is three feet below the surface of alpine flowers at your elbows. On the meadows where you begin dozens of tiny ponds, twenty to forty feet across, a scattering of mirrors, reflect flowers and peaks, reminding me of the ancient bronze mirrors in the Japanese museums. A mirror lures you to behold what is reflected in it, and you become reflective about the image, a symbol for self-reflective evaluation. I recall Thoreau's chapter, ''The Ponds,'' in *Walden*. So the pilgrims and I meditate about the moral character of our lives on this long ascent into the mists around the peak.

> Meadow pond mirrors
> On the slopes of Mt. Gassan
> Give reflection birth

At the top stands a sacred shrine, goal of the pilgrims, encased in thick stone walls against winter storms. I enter the crooked passageway, eyes alert so as not to offend those who come to worship. I hear the priest chanting, the bell ringing, drum beating, ending with the double clap of hands by all, a Shinto ritual, speaking to the spirits of the dead. The pilgrims this morning are poor people. Somehow Shugendo speaks to them. Just how I don't know. The Buddhism in Shugendo is a far-away

cousin to Buddha. Ascetic practices may put the ego to rout but
can they transform it, truly enlighten it? The point is not to kill the
ego but cure it of attachment.

Bashō writes about the beautiful lagoon and islets north of
Kisagata, later transformed by an earthquake in 1804 into a
marsh. He turned south at this point while we continue north to
Oga peninsula, seeking a secluded beach at Toga. A Japanese
high school teacher of English whom we met on the train helped
us telephone a small inn for reservations. A bond was struck
among us that led to a visit to Shoko Ono's home in Akita when we
returned from Toga, fortunately at festival time. Her interpreta-
tions added greatly to our understanding. In the Akita Museum
we saw the splendid large mural, ''The Seasons,'' by the
Japanese impressionist painter Fujita.

> Balancing tall poles
> Whose tips gay plumage adorned
> Fujita palette

It is not yet mid-morning and we are seated atop of Mt. Iwaki,
another sacred mountain; below the coast line of the Sea of Japan
curves in a graceful arc northward forming the Tsugaru peninsula.
Does Mt. Iwaki, like Mt. Chokai, cast its shadow on the sea at
dawn? It could. Dawn light on the peak lured us early from our
ryokan, the air already promising a hot summer day. Perspiring,
we bathed in a small cascade, totally refreshed and transformed.
Such icy stream-baths are a ritual delight in our hiking, purifying
and energizing us. We found few pilgrims at the summit where
the shrine contains a figure with a long pointed beard, Chinese
style, carved of black stone. Rare it is to find the doors of a Shinto
shrine open.

> Iwaki mountain
> Mates with the Sea of Japan
> Shinto Shrine open!

Still gazing at the sea coast I am fascinated by the various
clouds forming from the moisture layers near the earth, cumulus
billows riding in from the sea, charcoal black flat clouds at eye
level, fleecy white clouds on top. My eyes follow nearby two tiger
swallowtail butterflies chasing each other in a mating dance,
ascending straight up, falling together, traveling across these
clouds.

Top of Iwaki
Every kind of cloud abounds
Swallowtails mating

From the top of the mountain you can see the land spread like
a topographical map. Dimpled with cumulus cotton balls much of
Aomori prefecture stretches below.

Iwaki summit
Spreading Aomori landscape
Cotton ball dappled

With the sacred Shinto bell ringing behind me as pilgrims pull
the rope, I drift into a reverie of my son Karl who died of cancer,
doze off, head pillowed on my knees, awakening into a new world
of thick swirling clouds. The land below has disappeared.

Iwaki adrift
Apple orchards disappear
Lost child reverie

Nature carves windows. On the Rikuchu coast Pacific surf
pounds against the jagged rocks, wearing away softer veins until a
crack opens in the rock and waves squeeze through, smoothing
and widening, shaping a window with a water sill. I climb down
five hundred steps at Kitayamazaki to sit before a window and
watch the seaweed streamers swirl back and forth as each wave
surges through the window. This rhythm is the breathing of the
sea, a life pulse that tranquilizes, soothes, until you breathe in
harmony with the swells, and it seduces like the singing of
Homeric sirens. Why not slip gently into the water and be gone?
I mount the many steps to retrieve my pack and trudge the
gravel road.

Matsushima is celebrated for its aesthetic perfection of natural
beauty. Bashō's description has made it immortal. In *The Narrow
Road to the Deep North* Matsushima is the aesthetic foundation to
the religious experience of Mount Gassan. When these two are
seen in proper relation, interdependently combined, we can
understand the unique flavor of Japanese culture. Naturally, our
anticipation on reaching Matsushima was keenly focused. The
islands, the bridge, the pines, the shape of the bay shore — we
looked with care. But it was difficult, in summer, to capture the
quiet loneliness I felt when reading Bashō. The crowds interfered

with our hoped-for immersion in this place. No poetic spirit moved me; Bashō was silent for another reason, but his companion Sora wrote:

> *Here at Matsushima,*
> *O wood thrush, the plumage of cranes*
> *Would add to your song.*

Nikko, gaudy glory of Japan, extravaganza of baroque temples. You may approach the royal way through a long avenue of tall cedars to the sacred bridge. Our route was more round-about — through a narrow lane, across a footbridge and stepping stones over the river from the Japan Youth Hostel where we stayed. But once within the precinct you flow with all tourists, overwhelmed by the ornate display of colors, the proliferation of details of design, the circus-like flavor of pedlars and hawkers with whistling birds and snow cones, the elaborate attention to ostentation for its sheer impressive power, nothing less lavish to honor its *shoguns*, rulers. In the main hall, Sambutsudo, are three Buddhas, Senju with a thousand arms, horse-headed Batou Kannon with ears painted red, and Amida with his thin black moustache and head of blue snails. I look deep into their eyes but see no enlightenment.

> Blue-colored snails on Amida's head
> Red ears on horse-headed Batou Kannon
> Thousand armed Senju makes me dizzy
> Nikko spectaculars
> Gaudy Buddhism
> Degenerate religion
> Sakyamuni moans
> Will not reincarnate

But Nikko has some hidden charms. Experience develops an intuitive sense for locating aesthetic joys. Across the river from the main precinct we climb the hill to Ritsu-in, meet no visitors, yet within stands a lovely Kannon Buddha, gracefulness in bronze. Walking on along the other side of the river we stumble on a lantern-like tombstone without rival in our wanderings. So excited am I by its proportions and design that I sketch it in my Journal for August 16, 1972. Seeing it makes the whole day glorious but the gods have yet another surprise. Around behind the little closed-up temple, beneath an overhanging cliff, stand six stone figures from the knees up, their heights arranged in a pleasing arc. Are their lower legs cut off or are they buried in rubble from the cliff? The outside figures have fine heads and drapery; their headdress suggests a Greek influence, and I imagine that the sculptor traveled far to the west, perhaps to Northwest India where such Greek influences remain. Shall I see his inspiration when I arrive there next spring?

How different to me the great Kamakura Buddha looks today from July 1957 when my freighter to Singapore stopped in Yokohama. Then I spent my day in Kamakura where thousands of tourists each with transistor radio and camera snapped a picture, walked quickly around, and departed radio to ear. This morning at nine there are fewer than a dozen people, and we sit quietly on a stone at some distance, gazing for a long time in rapture. An early morning shower has left a dark wet pattern down the folds of drapery, over his stomach, through his folded hands, down the folds over his crossed legs, a few drops still dripping down. How natural to have a stream running over Buddha like the snails on his head.

> Early morning rain
> Wets the folds of Buddha's gown
> Riverlets run down

In a temple nearby you can see a tall standing Hase Kannon Buddha in an earthquake-proof vault, a graceful bronze figure set behind a cluttered altar, difficult to see from the rickety wooden anteroom, an aesthetic incongruity that disturbs me.

> Graceful free Kannon
> Bolted in earthquake-proof stance
> New liberation

Do you think the lords of Hades could be beautiful? Go at once to Enno-ji. Inside awaiting you are nine such lords, beautifully carved by Koyu in the twelfth century, fierce figures, eyes glaring, mouths twisted, eyebrows arched in rage, all made to frighten you into a better life, yet somehow moving.

> Carved by Koyu
> Nine fierce lords of Hades
> Eyebrows arched in rage

Our feet grow weary walking, our eyes are tired too. Late afternoon at Kencho-ji we step into a Buddha hall and see two young women napping. I sit to write some notes. Suddenly the great drum in the corner thunders, a priest shoos out the sleepers, turns off the lights, slams shut the great doors. Buddha almost smiled.

At Futamigaura near Ise Shrine the sun rises between two holy rocks, Izanagi and Izanami, male and female primogenators of the Japanese people and land. How do two insignificant rocks jutting out of the water just off shore come to be the most holy place in Japan? Did some ancient priest, blinded by seeing the sun rise between them, suffer a vision? Is that sufficient? At dawn we are there with hundreds of pilgrims to see the day recreated once more. Their holy observance is so simple, two claps of the hands and a slight bow with the head, a very brief prayer, no priest needed, no ceremony of any sort. The ancestor worship of Shinto is pure simplicity, a tiny child can learn to clap twice and pull the bell rope. Since everyone will die and become an ancestor, in effect, you pay reverence to yourself. Perhaps this explains the humanistic qualities I feel in the people at the Shinto Shrines.

Once when I was hiking along an old trail in the mountains I came upon a little Shinto shrine. Their doors are usually shut. At any larger shrine a fence or two encloses the inner building that sets behind an outer building where the bell rope hangs. At Ise there are three great fences blocking your vision of anything within. What is the great mystery within? Does a spirit reside there so potent no one can witness it? Perhaps I learned the answer from my little shrine, for when I opened the door all was revealed in the emptiness. Have they recognized that life returns to the great nothingness from which it came? For nothingness is always present, surrounds us with calm and quiet, absorbs into itself everything, every past life comfortably resides there, a perfect receptacle for all our ancestors, never over-crowded, vast and pervasive, hearing and absorbing every hand clap. Shinto states this truth boldly, unabashedly, and reaps a warm humanity. Buddhism comes to the same conclusion, for the nirvana achieved in liberation means literally ''to be blown out,'' another way of expressing our re-absorption into the vast nothing. And since it is nothing, we can have nothing to fear, nothing to gain. Take your life into your own hands and travel on. We shall sail to Java.

Java between Sea Voyages

We sailed from Kobe, Japan at 9 p.m. All night long I have been gently rocked in the cradle of sea swells, a motion that soothes me in some inner recesses of my body. Pre-dawn pink awakens me in some telepathic way, and I scurry to our window to check this light signal that governs the beginning of my days. I dress warmly and mount the top deck to watch dawn colors form and fade. The haze burns brighter where the sun will rise. At six sharp the red ball emerges from the sea burning a hole in the haze.

In an age of air travel, swift and precise in schedule, we prefer to go by ship with the leisure to reflect, to sift the experience of preceding weeks, to read travel accounts of places on further shores, preparing ourselves for the visions we will see. In the forward and sideward rolling motion of the swells I feel the living pulse of the sea, a water heartbeat, a rate harmonious to my own. We are aboard the Polish Ocean Lines freighter *Jurata,* a new ship bound for Hong Kong and then Singapore.

Yesterday I watched the winches and cranes hum and swing the cargo on. Still buried in my psyche is the fascination every child knows for the building crane or diesel shovel, bewitching in the precision of pinpoint lifts and drops, combining horizontal, vertical, diagonal forces, a skill of praxis by unknowing followers of Euclid. Soft things in sacks and cardboard cartons are lifted in rope nets. Hard goods have cables slipped around them. Stevedores in groups of six for each hoist demonstrate their geometric skill by placing cargo in the holds, sometimes heaving cartons dexterously into slots of that exact size. Watch any workers and you'll see age-old techniques unrecorded in any manual, the young watching the old without any words of instruction. But it is also infinitely dull work, the same motions performed day after week after year until the body gives out or retirement forces cessation and the greater boredom of nothing to do. I see all this as the winches wind up greased cables on their drums. Human existence is unfortunately divided according to whether creativity plays a part in thinking and imagination.

Buried in the bowels of the ship is a gigantic diesel engine turning the thick shaft and screw. Once the hawser ropes are thrown free from the wharf, a steady vibration of the entire ship, of every part, throbs with unrelieved persistence. This is the living pulse of the mechanical ship, the breathing of the diesel valves. I become especially aware of it when I lie down to sleep. My own body motions cease while the bed, firmly attached to the floor and the wall, transmits to me the rapid continuous shudder. I like the combination of the heartbeat of the sea and the steady shake of the engine.

When does the dawn begin? How late does day last? I am on the top deck when the stars still shine but there is a faint light in the east. The stars fade out, only the morning star shines bright in our wake as we sail toward the coast of China. The double dawn colors I've noticed while camping also occur at sea, an earlier display of deep orange-pink followed by a fading of color, then a second brilliant light show just before the sun rises. If the sea is calm all colors are intensified by the reflection of the sky in the sea. Light beams piercing the broken clouds on the horizon streak the water surface pink and silver-white. These last two dawn touches on the canvas are the brush strokes of Neptune dressing at dawn. They woo the sailor as the sirens did Ulysses' crew. Dawn begins when you are conscious of these color pageants. For some there is no dawn, only the morning.

In the darkness of waning night at 4 a.m. I slip out of bed as I hear the gangway being made ready for the pilot who will guide the ship into Hong Kong. The romance of an unknown port, the lure of a harbor made long ago. Gail wakens quickly, and from the top deck we watch the bright orange full moon setting behind the hills that surround the beautiful Hong Kong harbor. From my shoulder bag I take pieces of cake and a Japanese pear stocked there last evening from the pantry. We munch these as the port and starboard channel lights slip by. The hills are now etched by the lights of houses where people are waking, and tall skyscrapers loom into form as day quickens. The pilot threads his way through a maze of freighters at anchor seeking out our buoy, number A-10 I note when we make fast. Breakfast intervenes with a new hot cereal — spaghetti in warm milk with sugar, surprisingly tasty, another Polish custom to add to our experience. I slip some slices of ship-baked bread into my bag, preparing for a day in the city, not knowing where we might wish a snack.

Ashore we stumble upon a small exhibit of photos by the government of China showing improvements of life in Tibet since the revolution. In conversation we learn that a movie will be shown in Kowloon in the evening presenting recent archeological discoveries throughout China. We have read brief reports of these in the press, purchase a book about them, and are delighted to see the full-length film. We sense the germination of a future journey to China to see these ruins. This is typical of how our travels begin.

South of Hong Kong we enter tropical seas marked by the appearance of flying fish.

> Flying fish appear today
> Gliding swiftly o'er the waves
> Splashing spent into the sea
> A fish that wants to be a bird
> To swim no more but fly in air.

Swiftly like the flying fish our freighter at twenty-two knots reaches that international crossroad of ships: Singapore, the Jewel of the East. Its harbor, snug and safe, offers rest to us in transit to Jogjakarta, Indonesia, a spiritual crossroads of Hinduism and Buddhism.

Jogjakarta in central Java lies midway between two of the most impressive archeological ruins in the world, Borobudur and Prambanan, Buddhist and Hindu. In the surrounding area are equally magnificent temple ruins that demonstrate a synthesis of these two religions with indigenous Javanese beliefs: Chandi Mendut, Chandi Kalasan, Chandi Plaosan and Chandi Sewu. Here for us was the jewel of Southeast Asia.

Barabodor — it has many spellings — took us by surprise; an architectural masterpiece from small details to overall symmetry.

It is a massive stone hemisphere, a monumental stupa hill, carved in exquisite detail on four ascending terraces capped by three levels of *dagobs* (small bell-shaped stupas) each hollow with a Buddha sitting in meditation within, surmounted finally by an octagonal base supporting a huge *dagob*. With rapture and delight we examine the low relief of a section of panels in all their human revelation — thighs, torsos, breasts, faces, drapery, necklaces, hair-styles. Different colored lichens, white, gold, black, have created additional striking contrasts. The carving is somewhat rough without the perfect finish of some Indian temples. In half a day under intense sunlight we are able to examine only a small section of panels on two terraces, while tourists "do it" in twenty minutes, up to the top, down again, some photos, and away in their taxi to Prambanan.

Another day at Borobudur begins at lunch with a papaya purchased in the village. We wash it with soap and water from our canteen, then I carefully insert the paring knife to a depth sufficient to pass the center axis, being careful not to slide it back and forth carrying outside bacteria inside but rather to draw it all around at exactly that depth laying open the two halves to eat with our own spoons. Such precautions are necessary in the tropics. Many such tricks we have in our travel kit. We lunch under the tree on the south side where one can view the entire stupa in its hemispherical form. From this position I can see one hundred Buddhas in their niches deep in meditation. I sit the same way meditating on this building.

I like to see the stone so carved that the flesh comes alive, dancers dance, animals run, walk and jump, lips smile. After an hour or more looking-in-joy at the relief, our aesthetic sense is satiated. We rest by climbing to the upper terraces of *dagobs*, leaving worldly things below for the purity of quiet forms, closer to nirvana. Our eyes relax in the distant vistas of mountains and valley, coconut palms and rice paddies, tobacco and cornfields. Great thunderheads grow, the sky darkens, showers cool the air.

> Borobudur
> Jewel on a hill in Java
> Five terraces of carved joy
> Stone come alive in human figures
> Silent music of stone-shaped bells
> A Buddha encased in each
> Seen through perforated stone

Hemisphere
Of cut stone blocks
Piled up around this hill
Carved in sculptural glory
Flecked with meditation cells
Four hundred Buddhas sit

Jataka tales
Scenes from Buddhist lore
Told in stone relief
As I circumambulate
Lured by sensuous dancers

Our daily rhythm takes us on alternate days to Prambanan, the Hindu Temple or to Chandi Mendut, a small temple combining Buddhist and Hindu religions. We ride the crowded, stuffy local buses with farmers and goods to and from market. For some unknown reason people do not like to open the windows, and we debark in a sweat. Never mind. For the best approach to Prambanan get off the bus at the bridge, half a mile before the town. From the bridge you'll see the Temple, a steep mountain in the plain, right in line with the river valley. On the west side a path follows the river affording continuous vistas of the temple. People are washing clothes, bathing themselves, brushing their teeth, drinking, playing, all within several hundred yards. The water flows clear around rectangular green beds of some water plant. Small dams carry it off into irrigation ditches.

Prambanan looms ever higher, specific carvings take on recognizable form. Climb the wall if you are inclined, that's the way the children go in and out. We do the same. Prambanan now towers over you, ten to twelve stories high. It sits on a platform in the form of a Greek cross with additional corners to increase the number of frontal panels facing you as you walk around its terraces. The outside wall of the terrace promenade is a frieze of dancers and musicians rather hard to see close up. I back off on a ledge just wide enough for my feet, marveling at the

33

lively rhythms caught in stone, sensuously excited by the human forms, draped only in thin ribbons that lend additional curves to the nude bodies. The corridor of perambulation offers you the stories from the *Ramayana* with all their richness of human life. In four chambers within some god attends you and you the god. Higher walls above the terrace are all carved until the steep pitch of the tower shoots skyward. On the tower tiers of *dagobs* (bell-shaped stupas) rise to the large *dagob* that caps the stone mountain. North and south of the main building stand two similar temples, not as high but of the same general design. East of each of these are the base platforms of ruined temples, perhaps of the same design, and surrounding this central courtyard were hundreds of small temples, each housing a meditation chamber about eight by eight feet in the same basic architectural form. One or two are restored to indicate the design. The whole complex in its original form was without rival in the world. Prambanan is a focal point of the spiritual world.

> Prambanan
> Approach northeast along the river
> Village folk in the clear running water
> Washing, fishing, bathing, drinking
> Bright-colored clothes drying on the grass
>
> Prambanan
> Focus of Javanese Hinduism
> Tiers of bells soaring skyward
> Each a miniature stupa
> Known as a *dagob* in Indonesian art
>
> Prambanan
> Pyramid of *dagobs*
> Set atop a Greek cross
> Architectural wonderpiece
> Ramayana panels in deep relief
> Frieze of dancers, rhythm in stone

In central Java a unique synthesis of Buddhist and Hindu architecture and sculpture occurred, sometimes the result of a Buddhist prince marrying a Hindu princess, producing a stone carved Buddha seated full lotus with beautiful breasts, Lakshmi incarnated as a bodhisattva. I see these life-size statues first at Chandi Plaosan, in a field of ruined temple stones a mile east of Prambanan, one hundred yards south of the principal temple.

Half a dozen such female Buddhas await you there, as striking a combination of Buddhist peace and Hindu creativity as can be seen in this world. You might not walk this hundred yards south unless your way of exploring ruins includes poking around the periphery of a temple. Gail and I delight in this discovery.

Chandi Plaosan seems to manifest the influence of Greek sculpture and architecture through the Gandhara culture. In each of the three rooms of Plaosan the wall contains carved panels to rival the finest art gallery, paintings in stone of exquisite delicacy, and on each altar life-size human figures with highly expressive faces. I lightly run my fingers over eyes, nose, lips. What a joy to be free to touch this sculpture, to caress these figures. I linger in these rooms reflecting on the sculptural odyssey I shall follow from Java to Greece. Surrounding this temple a graveyard of stones awaits reconstruction. I imagine it complete — a harmonious combination of rectangular forms and pyramidical dome decorated with *dagobs*. Guarding the gates of Plaosan are eight-foot guardian figures holding heavy clubs, muscles rippling, poised to strike. For me, they link Java to Japan where similar guardian figures stand watch at Buddhist temple gates. What is their common origin?

> Chandi Plaosan
> Buddhist-Hindu-Javanese wonder
> Touched somehow by Greek Gandhara
> Stone relief panels of standing bodhisattvas
> Swinging one hip high to catch your eye
> A lotus blossom offered in the left hand
> Four bells hung around the head
> A short skirt of four horizontal ribbons
> Her head tilts to nod to you
> Enter here for paradise

Close by in a cluster of five houses made of bamboo sides and thatched roofs I see a small girl lower the well bucket attached to the end of a forty-foot bamboo pole hinged to a second bamboo pole that teeters up and down weighted with a rock at the opposite end. Up comes the full bucket. A middle-aged woman, bare-breasted, dumps it over her head, soaks her skirt. Cooled, she ties the end of a fifteen-foot long waist band, fifteen inches wide, to a bamboo tree and slowly wraps it round her waist by turning herself round and round approaching the tree; the joy of feeling slim and cool.

On the way to Borobudur you change to a local bus at Muntilan. Stroll through the lively rural market. No supermarket stocks as much variety of all one's needs and wants. Dodge the duck flocks, watch the blacksmith shape a hoe, select a conical straw hat. When you hear the bus horn, swing aboard, and ask the driver to drop you at Chandi Mendut.

I watch some children at play under a fruit tree, one climbing high in the branches to pluck the most delicious fruit, another shinnying up the trunk, yet another riding horseack on his playmate in the shade. Amazed and delighted, I discover a carved panel in the entrance way that depicts exactly these activities watched over by the goddess Hariti nursing a child. Converted by Buddha, this she-devil formerly ate children. Inside sit three of the most beautifully carved human-shaped gods in the world. The center Buddha has both legs hanging down instead of crossed in the common lotus position. On each side sit two female bodhisattvas with the outside leg down, the inner one up. Their faces are powerfully serene.

Three outside walls of this temple have carved relief panels, tapestries in stone combining living shapes with formal floral patterns. In the late afternoon we sit in the shade of a large banyan tree eating fresh papaya, lost in reverie contemplating these carved walls, sun shadows etching their contours, accenting the many forms.

Chandi Mendut
Carved stone tapestries on each wall
Floral border ascends into Kala's face
Relief columns frame each panel
While two attendant bodhisattvas
Serve the four-armed Buddha

Chandi Mendut
Walk up between the massive balustrades
To see the entrance panel where children play
Climb a tree, ride another horseback
While Hariti takes care, a child at her breast
Who formerly ate children
Before the Buddha taught her

Chandi Mendut
Massive sculptured figures sitting inside
The master with both feet on the floor
Mounted on a Greek-like pedestal
Female attendants let only one leg down
A trinity of stone gods beyond compare

From one temple to another we prefer to ride in a two-wheeled horse-drawn cart, the local mode of transportation, often sharing our ride with several peasant women, free of the crowded dusty bus, moving at a slow pace, allowing time to see details of village life. In Jogjakarta we ride in bicycle rickshaws, the common taxi throughout the Orient, quiet, smog-free, slow-paced, cooled by the breeze of its gentle motion. In Japan the auto taxi has replaced the cycle rickshaw, creating smog and noise intolerable to life. I see no gain from this speed. Another day we jog along to Chandi Sewa and Chandi Kalasan, temples on the road to Prambanan.

The crucial importance of seeing ruins a second or third time demonstrates its truth today on a return visit to Kalasan. There the god Kala stares down at you from over the four doorways; his eyes glare at you in a strange way since his eyes have no pupils, a vacant glance, while in other carvings he has a double pupil, one inside another, that bores within your consciousing. A pilgrim reaching Kalasan confronts the god of introspective reflection. Know thyself before you can return his stare. Is there some relation between this powerful glance and the use of octagonal shapes throughout the design of the building? Imagine those eight sides as mirrors reflecting within. The ground plan is a Greek cross to which has been added a smaller corner between two larger corners providing additional panels for carving in relief. The crowning *dagob* on top is octagonal as are the bases of columns. If you draw a line from the tips of the larger corners you form an octagon (see previous sketch). I feel this clearly as I contemplate its overall form.

I find here in the deep niches over the north and south door-ways the full lotus female buddha of Plaosan. Who is she? Also delightful is the floral pattern in reversing curve as a border around the great panels. And if you have an eye attuned to the pro-file of mouldings, an aesthetic motif I discovered from persual of my father's architectural books and renderings, Kala-san will excite you. The large flat vertical area in the middle of the profile is a carved relief floral frieze running around the entire building except for the four stair-ways up to the entrances over which Kala glares down.

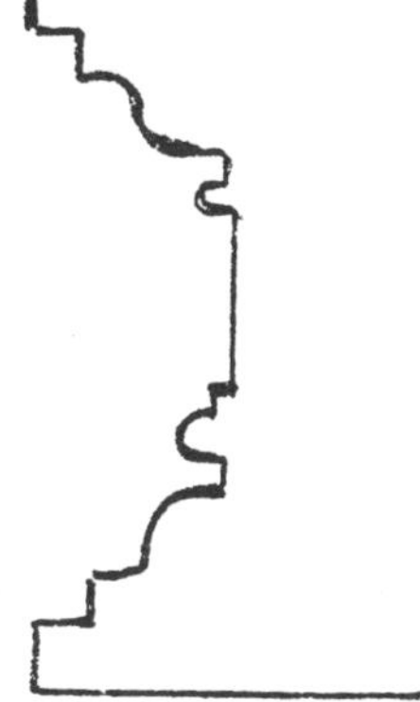

Chandi Kalasan
Where god Kala glares down on you
From over all four doorways
Great eyes without pupils
Disturb my visions
Some eyes with double pupils
Bore into inner thoughts
Octagonal motifs blend forms together
Female buddhas full lotus in deep niches
I wonder who they are and where from

From Java we flew to Singapore to meet our ship for Madras. The Bay of Bengal is much too large to be called a bay. How did it come by this name? It is properly a sea adjacent to an ocean. Four days we sailed aboard the *State of Madras* to cross it. Some six hundred Indians from Singapore, Port Klang and Penang are aboard, mostly bunk and deck passengers, perhaps fifty in first and second-class cabins. Deck space is not an accommodation you find on a fancy cruise ship. It enables poor Indians to travel home from work in Malaya. Every square inch of deck is used. You claim an area equal to your straw sleeping mat, say three by six feet with a metal trunk or bundle at the head. Two floors below the deck are filled as well as the deck itself. Bunk passengers are in triple-tiered wooden bunks, perhaps twenty-one to thirty people in a room, no mattress furnished, stuffy and hot. Deck passengers have more space overhead and can enjoy the starlit sky. How so many live so close with such neatness and cleanliness is striking, an impressive cultural trait.

Quietly reading in a deck chair I look up to watch flying fish scatter out of the way of the ship. Overhead black coal smoke streams astern, blocking the sun with flickering shadows on the deck that go dancing off across the sea. Suddenly the calm surface ripples, black clouds loom ahead, a squall drops rain. As suddenly a strange rainbow literally grows out of the sea, the bow of colors coming into being clockwise in a low thick arc across the sea, splashing down onto the water where the colors run together. So low, so thick, so short an arc, created clockwise before my eyes is a new wonder in my experience. The primary colors — red, yellow, blue — form thick bands with slight orange and green between.

Along the coast of India from Nagapattinam north to Madras the fishermen, singly or in pairs, brave the sea in small boats constructed of five curved solid logs lashed together, constantly awash with water, fitted with a curved-up bow sprit to break the waves. Deftly they work their nets for small fish that they store in baskets lashed to the logs. Such boats must be as old as dug-out logs, a sea-craft unchanged over millennia.

As the long evening stretches to midnight, one by one, lighthouses on the coast guide our way until a long arc of streetlights marks the Marina of Madras, a road we last strolled along years ago. A cascade of memories sweeps over us, broken by the rattle of the anchor chain at 1 a.m. announcing the end of our sea voyage.

India: Sculptural Paradise

In the experience of returning to a place you love, to a place that has dramatically changed and formed your life, the traveler faces an adventure of unknown responses. Did I idealize it in memory? How will it have changed? Is my life open to further change from its power? Madras is such a place for us.

Our excitement and anticipation peaked as we leaned on the ship's rail while the great hawsers were made fast, the gangway swung into place. Packs on our backs, arms and legs free, we descended, quickly passed through customs, bargained for a cab, and let our eyes roam the streets, each silent, wrapped in impressions, till we arrived at our hotel. Soon we were free to stroll in familiar places conversing about our perceptions: more street noise from traffic, more people friendly in the lovable Indian way, more dust swirling, bookshops yielding prizes as of old. In the three-wheeled open pedi-cab we darted in and out of traffic between lorries and buses towering over us, seeking news of a dear friend Gail had lost touch with. Over brahmin coffee at her father's house we were given an address for a small town, Kuzhithurai, in southern Tamil Nadu. Days in the Madras Museum once again roused our aesthetic delight with the sensuous charm of temple sculpture, the exquisite perfection of Indian bronzes and those wheel-shaped dancing *natarajas* beyond compare. Nearby at the Das Prakash Hotel were tasty brahmin vegetarian meals at the long tables, waiters with their brass pots and ladles, offering more rice, *dhal, pappadum.* So began a sculptural ecstasy that spread across our months in India. Later we will know the effects of our returning.

South of Madras stand the incredible monolithic stone temples of Mamallapuram. Imagine a building of solid stone the size of a house. What an adventure for architecture! In November 1957 we walked together here. The photo on the cover of my last book, *Rebelling, Loving and Liberation,* is a couple in stone from here. By moonlight the first night we strolled down the beach to the Shore Temple. Silently, the resting stone bullocks on the outer wall surround the sleeping Vishnu inside, one arm thrown back, relaxed, over his head. A priest with oil lamp illuminates his figure, adding black smoke soot to the ceiling. The prospect of soft moonlight on the stone lures us on to view Arjuna's Penance: the life-sized elephants come alive. Great vitality and artistic talent joined together with the political order and religious fervor of the Pahlava culture over a thousand years ago to create these monuments; here is *The Wonder That Was India,* as in the title of A. L. Basham's definitive work. How are today and yesterday linked? Hinduism continues to excite and hold the people. How? Do these temples show an answer?

In the dawn as the sun rises out of the sea, we are again at the Shore Temple, watching the breakers crash against the stone wall and throw white spray into the air to shower down on the giant lingam before the temple. What an orgasm of delight I feel. Pilgrims are here for a ritual bath at dawn in the sea: men strip to their loin cloths, women deftly manage their saris, reverently they enter the temple. On the equinox when the sun's shadow from the lingam falls on the seated Siva and Parvati, creation is celebrated.

> Two green parrots perched atop the Shore Temple
> Dawn sun touching Parvati who sits on Siva's thigh
> Full moon last night softening the stone
> Raucous calls and flashing green as parrots fly
> Pilgrims bathe in ritual purity
> Creation begins anew with every dawn
> Thousands of dragonflies sport in rock-reflected heat
> Reclining Vishnu relaxed in contemplation

By moonlight and sunlight, or wet with the gently falling rain, we go several times to see Arjuna's Penance, a vast deep relief carving including the whole creation of gods, humans and animals. In the center is a crevasse where the mighty Ganges flows, life-giving holy water of India. A man in Delhi once told me that in chemical tests its water killed harmful germs. With all the created things Arjuna offers penance. The sculptural work is perfect in its natural depiction of animals and the heavenly forms of gods. I feel a balance of figures in their living sizes harmoniously distributed, no detail lacking.

> Two giant elephants alive in stone
> Ear about to flap away a fly
> His trunk might squirt, watch out
> Pairs of Apsaras sailing in the air
> Three cobras whose open hoods shelter gods
> Ascend the mighty Ganges whose holy waters cure
> Lions, monkeys, deer, turtles, lizard, hare
> Join Arjuna in his penance, their
> Vital organs worn smooth from touch of hands —
> Cow's teats, breasts, Nandi's balls, baby Krishna
> To touch is not forbidden in this land

In the sunny afternoon Gail and I walk around the hill to visit the rock-carved cave-temples. Coming to the temple of the elephant-god Ganesh who do we find but the same holy man we met years ago, caring for the god and blessing those who stop at this shrine. Deaf now, he recognized us, smiled deeply, touched our foreheads with white rice powder. Across the years he has cared for Ganesh while we sought liberation in many lands, in books and art. Perhaps his way brings peace. Why were we drawn back?

But the temple of temples for me is Varaha Mandapam where the inside left panel shows Lakshmi who captivates all those who love to love.

> Lakshmi at Varaha Mandapam
> Attended on each side by a graceful woman
> Cunts blackened with ritual candle smoke
> Breasts rubbed smooth by a million caresses
> Two elephant heads to guard them
> Lakshmi sits with knees spread apart
> I place jasmine petals between her thighs

As the sun sets, we climb to a high point on the ridge with a full view of ocean, sky, bay, rice paddies and town to witness a festival of colors on this holiday evening of the Hindu Festival of Lights, locally called Kartihe. For an hour we gaze upon the sun's magic canvas, the changing contrasts of pink, gold, orange, silver, gray and turquoise — shifting, melting, mixing. My eyes are in an ecstasy. All the while iridescent green swallows swoop and sing, catching insects, cavorting in the air, dressed beautifully with a black eye stripe, brown head cap, black band on the rear edge of the wings, and a single long needle-like tail feather. When the last colors fade we descend to the village where candle lights are burning before the homes. Leading across the porch and into the house curves a patch bordered by candle lights, small clay dishes with oil and wick. Between each pair of candles on the floor is a white star-shaped geometric design made by spreading rice powder in a metal pan whose bottom is perforated with tiny holes. You place it gently on the floor, tap it, lift it up and a star is born. After greetings in Tamil we enter, accept sweet cakes, feel their joyous holiday spirit. A brother calls his sister Lakshmi, and I feel the whole day culminate in Lakshmi's power.

Climbing up the metal ladder on the rear of the local bus, I hoist our packs, one by one, to the luggage rack covering the roof, tying them in place against the rutted roads amidst bundles and packages, trunks and baskets, learning a maneuver that becomes a bodily habit in the months ahead. We journey to Koncheepuram, capital of Pahlava kings to study temples there.

Before you enter these living religious sanctuaries you must remove your shoes while those who go barefoot through the streets deposit inside whatever clings from outside since they have no shoes to remove. I wear my socks to intercept what I can, noting once again the strange cultural variations that constitute being clean. Our English word 'temple' fails to communicate the size, majesty and complexity of buildings and activities that we visit within a South Indian temple-compound of the Dravidian style. Typically they occupy a single city block but some extend over five city blocks. Rising high over the entrance is a high tower of steep pyramidical form elaborately carved, called a *gopuram*. As we stroll inside the compound around the main temple, usually dedicated to a particular deity, minor temples or shrines offer us a pantheon of gods and goddesses sacred to Hinduism. A pond, called a tank, rectangular in shape, perhaps fifty by eighty feet, has sides of sloping steps descending into the water, where ritual bathing for purification takes place. At any time of the day we see a dozen worshipers bathing. Our human cleanliness symbolizes religious purity.

Ascending a few steps we enter the *mandapam*, a pillared hall where worshipers gather before making their devotions to a deity in the sanctuary, known as a *vimana*. These two buildings may be connected. In other parts of the compound, we encounter shops for religious articles, living quarters for the priests, kitchens and storage areas for temple carts used in processions. Between the buildings we meander over stone-paved courtyards offering us views of the elaborate, exquisite carving that covers the building. This profusion of carving symbolizes the ceaseless creativity of Hindu belief, and the variety of subject matter manifests the idea of inclusiveness central to Hinduism. Here at Koncheepuram we begin our exploration of all these elements in various stages of development, for the city contains about a dozen temple-compounds, small and large.

The sculpture of Koncheepuram temples offers a stylization that moves ever further from the natural toward the grotesque. The remains of painted plaster over the stone strike me as more grotesque than the stone shapes beneath. Is there an inverse relation between the degree of formalized religious symbolism and the naturalness of its sculpture, the ritualized stereotypes giving rise to formalized un-natural sculpture?

With the coolness of sunset we ramble to Ekambaranath Temple with its celebration of creative-sexual power, hundreds of linga and in the innermost shrine a special lingam smoothed and oiled for the gods. High up on a pillar a woman spreads her legs and with both hands on her thighs she fingers herself, an expression of creative ecstasy. On another pillar a man stands with a fine stiff cock in both his hands. Here all is readiness, the creative power of sexual joy receives religious sanctification whereas elsewhere such portraiture is taboo. Although most cultures are puritanical in their sexual mores, this one allows full depiction in religious buildings while others do not. I puzzle over this.

Next day, returning from another temple, we espy the wheels of a gigantic temple cart, ten feet in diameter. We know from pictures that these would support a cart fifty to sixty feet high. Wouldn't you be awed to see the god taken out in a procession, brilliantly costumed and painted, cleverly lit by candles behind? You might reconsider your evil deeds.

From around the world many pilgrims come to Pondicherry to visit Aurobindo's Ashram, inspired by his writings translated into many tongues, tongues we hear in these streets as we stroll to meals at the Ashram, cafeteria style, vegetarian, wholesome, tasty, clean. Many seekers meet here, following freely diverse forms of meditation. You are free to find your own way amongst a great variety of activities or studies. Aurobindo's grave may move you. There is a silent power there. I like to watch the people come and go, each with their own distinctive attitudes of reverence and inspiration befitting many cultures touched by Aurobindo's wisdom. Nearby is the architectural inspiration of Auroville still in its early stages of construction but the models of the buildings are breath-taking. Will it come to be?

On the local bus from Pondicherry to Chidambaram, passengers have their market baskets, hens and children, sleeping rolls and fresh produce. As likely as not there is no glass in the windows. What need of it in such tropical warmth? Instead a rolled-up canvas can be dropped in rain. We pass between flat rice fields in their special shades of green in different stages of growth bordered by coconut palms whose fronds shape a sphere, a cluster of nuts tucked just beneath. Villagers transplant the rice or weed in water up to their knees, men in loin cloths, lithe and supple, women in bright-colored saris folded up and tucked in at the waist, one shoulder bare, bending rhythmically. Others are busy threshing rice on concrete platforms where a bullock walks in circles dragging a log roller to knock out the rice kernels. The edges of the pavement may be lined with drying rice for a mile. Indian highways serve in ingenious ways. A few wells have diesel pumps but most are worked by a bullock who walks all day in a circle turning a shaft connected to a rope loop with a dozen wooden buckets that dip up water and tip to spill into a trough leading to the field. A village street has neat manure piles, and the "tanks" remind me of our farm pond at home. In the tank everything is washed handsomely clean, beginning with the bullocks, affectionately scrubbed, then the saris and other garments, pounded on rocks to loosen the dirt. Finally, the people at the end of the day's toil wash themselves for supper and sleep, gossiping all the while. Washing and bathing is a ritual of Hindu life, a symbol of purity daily enacted.

In the ancient temple city of Chidambaram we stay in the guest hostel of Annamalai University where Gail studied Tamil in 1963-64. I knew Annamalai only from her letters. Now I want my feet to feel the paths she tread, see the vistas she holds in memory, so that some parts of our separate pasts are shared in present experience, creating larger and deeper intimacy. This is an important facet of our Indian journey. Travel is a way two persons grow together.

Evening temple bells call us from our room, out the compound gate, along the packed earth street. In the temple a dozen people, villagers and students, come to worship Siva and Parvati, seated side by side. Gay music of adoration from a drum and a clarinet-like reed instrument, a *nadaswaram*, reverberate in a lively rhythm, minor chords punctuating points of the ritual. A friendly university student explains the ceremony. We find an intimacy in this local temple and an ease in being here, uncrowded and accepted, perhaps accepted because it is near the University from which visitors have come before.

Another day we are off by horse-drawn jutka cart to the renowned temple of Nataraja in nearby Chidambaram. Within the temple I feel an artistic imbalance: religious ritual triumphs over aesthetic form. Finely-carved statues are blocked by a cluttered altar. High on the gopuram towers, weeds grow in the plaster coating over the stone carving; their roots will soon crack off the plaster. Inside, a two-story colonnade with a delicate carved railing has fallen into disrepair. Worshipers stop to see what interests us. Every day they have passed this spot on their way to make obeisance in hope of a better life, to perform a ritual they have been taught. How, I wonder, did the original designer succeed in balancing art and religion in the temple design? Was appreciation any greater in the past? When the great temples were built in the flowering of Hinduism, the fullest possible celebration of the deities was created by using every art form. Later, in the long practice of religion a slow degeneration of this complex artistic celebration narrowed the focus to the simplest ritual forms while all else was progressively neglected. This narrowing heralds a decrease in cultural energies: a peak has passed in the rhythms of civilized achievements. The contrast disappears where temples have become archeological buildings because no one worships there and all ritual has been removed. Only artistic preservation remains.

Hinduism in India provides a unique example of the long survival of a religion with a vitality sufficient to sustain its practices so that they do not become archeological exhibits, yet not sufficient to energize new artistic celebration. The Mayan temples in Yucatān are an example of another route history follows: archeological and artistic preservation, but lifeless. In a conversation with the four teachers in the Philosophy Department at Annamalai, I notice a parallel confinement of energy to only two Indian movements of thought, Saiva Siddhanta and Aurobindo. The full celebration of the Indian tradition, much less of the world, is not present.

As we watch the sunset from the roof of our hostel, the sun's rays catching the yellow blossoms of a tree below whose fragrance fills the air, a black goat hops the wall and begins to eat each yellow blossom that has fallen on the lawn. He nips them up daintily, perhaps three dozen in all. What a glorious color he is inside. If you are not a vegetarian and taste his mutton, what delicate flavor will it have? Goats have been known to eat many strange things, some not so dainty. This one is indeed fastidious, not merely a vegetarian but a blossom-arian. Charles Doughty in his *Travels in Arabia Deserta* remarks how the flavor of camel's milk varies depending on the diet, and we know how the taste of honey changes depending on the flowers visited, and how the taste of vegetables depends on the soil they were grown in. So let us feed ourselves the purest most sublime things and we shall become as pure in our being. Spirit and food are so closely linked we can say that what we are is what we eat. I shall try flower blossoms. Are Indian people so beautiful because they are vegetarians?

If someone tells you of a small out-of-the-way temple with fine sculpture, be sure to go. By jeep over rough dirt bullock-cart roads we journey to the village of Melakkadambur, west of Chidambaram, to the small temple called Amirtha Gadaiswarar. The sculpture, in a hard fine-grained bluish stone, an unusual color in itself, is exquisite, dancing figures in rare poses, sensuous and lively; larger god-figures in quiet poise, wise and concerned. The priest takes some rags off several goddesses, heavenly to behold, telling us that women should be clothed. We wonder why dancers are left unadorned. A six-inch frieze at waist height runs around the entire temple, depicting the totality of life and imagination. Inside is as fine a bronze *Nataraja* as can be found in the Madras Museum, but here it is in its rightful setting. I wonder what is needed to revitalize India today, to regain this celebration of the totality of existing. Gandhi tried to re-evoke it but Nehru took the path of western nationalism, industrialization and technology.

One of the great temple cities of south India is Thanjavur, the British called it Tanjore, with the massive single *gopuram* (tower) of the Great Temple centering and guiding the life of the city. In the northwest corner of the temple-compound is the small temple of *Subrahmanya Kovil*, shrine of Kartikkeya, son of Siva, an architectural gem of proportion and detail. Tiny carvings dance with life, moulding profiles catch our eye. We wonder why the larger sculptures of gods are often in a fine-grained polished stone. A circular carved disk shows a female figure with arms around a lingam, and in another a cow licks the lingam. These are choice. High up on the west side is a woman seated with her arms around her drawn-up knees, head resting on her knees for a pillow. In contrast to this naturalistic perfection designs on the columns portray mythical ideas in a baroque pitch. Relief models of many temples are arrayed around the building — here is a book of south Indian temple designs. The elephants that form the bannister rails literally lift us up the stairway into the sanctum. If beauty is truth we had best enter in.

Another great temple city — Madurai, the home of many Indian friends, Gail's home in 1955-58. Our pleasure is to stay at the home of Vasanthi and Venkitaraman and their sons Ashok and Anand. The traveler's delight is to unpack and settle for awhile, to catch the aroma of fresh-ground Indian coffee served Brahmin style with milk on first awakening in the morning. Vasanthi prepares delicious Tamil dishes: *dosai*, a thin dough of rice flour and black gram, fried like a pancake; *iddli*, a muffin-like cake of rice and black gram steamed and served with coconut chutney; *appam*, a delicate, coconut-flavored sweet rice cake, spongy in the center, thin around the edges.

Long before dawn we awake to the deafening blare of cinema

music from loud speakers in celebration of a religious festival. Seeking quiet, we bicycle into the country east of the city, past a small lake, the road full of people on their way somewhere. Elephant Hill dominates the landscape ahead, its red sandstone catching the sunrise. At the outlet of the lake, the water cascades over rocks. In the pools bathers purify their bodies before going to the shrine, fifteen-foot long saris streaming in the current or waving in the air drying, one end wrapped once around the bather for modest cover. How fine to see the human form revealed, the shining muscular backs of men, the long wet black hair of the women flowing like a sari in the current. Standing in the stream facing the rising sun a young man prays with hands together over his head, eyes shut. He has washed and now turns inward to his spirit.

Returning, we meet an increasing flow of traffic, on foot, cycling, in two-wheel carts, bicycle rickshaws, a worn-out taxi or two, and local buses. The breeze is fresh, the songs of birds fill the air. Hinduism has a vitality that sustains but doesn't create. Is this the immortality of a religion? Ritual practiced so long becomes frozen in forms that block artistic creativity. I see a parallel to this in the history of Indian Philosophy wherein no new developments have emerged in recent centuries with the possible exceptions of Aurobindo and Gandhi, yet there are brilliant minds like Radhakrishnan and Dasgupta.

In the city once more we find the dirt street swept clean and dampened before each gate or doorway upon which a white rice powder geometrical design, often of high complexity, makes holy the entrance to that home. Why doesn't such aesthetic sensitivity and artistic creativity appear in new temple construction?

In the evening twilight, I watch the gathering of water bearers at the tap in the street filling large brass pots, burnished bright, so shaped to rest upon your hip with an arm encircling the concaved neck or set on a cloth coil atop your head balanced effortlessly. Their lively conversation is an evening newspaper, no printing press needed. The tap runs constantly as each washes and shines the outside of her pot with ashes, rinses inside and fills. When each house has its own water pipes this social comraderie will disappear, isolation and alienation of household labor will increase. The village well is not just a source of water but a communal bond.

Our guide on many Madurai excursions is M. Natarajan, poet and businessman, lover of temple art and patient, understanding friend. He escorts us through the labyrinth of Meenakshi Temple, leads us up the winding stairway inside the tower-*gopuram* and out the tiny trap door on to the highest crest. One day we had our lunch sandwiches and tangerines there, roof-tops spreading away in all directions, the temple tank crowded round with ritual bathers, the sky-thrust of the other three *gopurams* crowning the four entrances facing each quadrant of the city. The interior halls of Meenakshi hold endless experiences, religious and artistic, humorous and pathetic. Another day at sunset we journey to Nagamalai Hill to see Jain caves and carving. We contemplate a full-breasted goddess mounted on a horse. After sunset, how pleasant to relax and talk in the cool breeze, watching it ripple the rice fields, weaving our excursions together with perceptive conversations. He loves his city and gives that love to his friends.

The traveler must be a thoughtful pragmatist, gauging the climate, terrain, accommodations, modes of transportation, allowing some weeks of experience in a country before completing one's gear. Before we left Madurai an essential item to obtain was a double-bed mosquito net of light weight to carry in our back packs. We want to have our arms free to swing aboard a bus or train and to allow us to walk a moderate distance. In the Madurai bus station once again I mount the ladder on the rear of the bus, pack on my back, climbing to the roof where I can lash our two packs in the racks, saving many bargaining sessions with porters and becoming self-sufficient for lonely country stops. We each carry a briefcase with notebooks, books, Journals, pens, pencils ready at hand for reading or writing as we wait or relax, catching fresh impressions before they escape.

At noon we stop off in the town of Kovilpatti on the main road south from Madurai. We find a simple accommodation in the municipal bungalow for water inspectors at the edge of town. The room is sparsely furnished, a single bed with mattress, no sheets or towels, a wooden chair and small table, a bathroom with a floor-level squat toilet "flushed" by pouring in a bucket of water, no shower or tub but a dipper and pail for bathing, concrete floors throughout, a comfortable building for a small town. We are happy to find it. We unfold our two bed sheets sewn together on three sides to make a bag, spread it on the mattress, suspend our mosquito net on long strings to any odd hook-point, carefully tuck in the edges all around the bed. Although it is December no blanket is needed in this warm climate.

Our destination, on a side road twelve miles west, is a small monolithic rock-cut temple above the village of Kalugumali, an exquisite stone gem Gail has visited twice before, a pilgrimage for us to see the sculpture, one photo of which has graced my desk for a decade. We find the entire village employed in making matches, the streets spread with matchboxes or match sticks drying in the sun. Women, children, men, all work, splitting, shaving, gluing, tipping the wood. School children follow us through the streets trying out their English phrases. Above the pond or tank on the edge of the village stands this small temple hewn out of the rock, creating a cleft in the ridge, carved from the top down as at Mamallapuram. It has a rectangular base with three tiers of relief sculpture, and an octagonal dome whose top culminates in an eight-petaled lotus. On the friezes you will find pot-bellied musicians to lure and soothe you, Kala-god figures with floral extremities, seated gods and goddesses in relaxed postures, a knee up, a leg down, tilted head, full lips, fine arched eyebrows, coils of carefully arranged hair, all in a craftsmanship of naturalistic perfection.

We lunch on the east side in the shade before Siva and Parvati, watching the bathers below in the tank; my eyes shift back and forth from carved figures to living bodies, a timeless harmony of then and now, gods and people. Two seated women in low relief have their backs facing out to you, heads turned profile facing each other, an unusual position but powerfully stated. On the west side, center section, two figures, male and female from the waist up, are floral designs below, not mermaids but floral-maids. Round and round we go as the sun's elevation changes the shadows and illumination, climbing up to touch and caress. Here is a masterpiece alone by a small village. Who was the architect, the sculptors? Why build it here?

Returning by the tank we are invited to bathe. In the village, children gaze at Gail's white skin and red hair, point at my hiking boots. All go with us to the bus stop, shouting and laughing, wonderfully friendly, a royal send-off. Back at the bungalow we bathe from a bucket of water using a dipper to pour over us; rinse, soap, rinse, one bucket will give a fine bath. We dry off by standing for evaporation coolness. Keep our towel clean for miles ahead. Stretch out nude on our cool sheet, tuck in the net, mosquito safe, asleep in the twilight. Reading lamps are not furnished.

The traveler may find a lost friend that letters fail to reach. Years of silence make one wonder if and where the person lives. In Madras we took a tiny three-wheeled "put-put" cab through dusty streets to the last known address of ten years ago. New buildings made it difficult to recognize the house, but an old shopkeeper recognized Gail and shortly Parameswari's father appeared. He invited us in, sent out for coffee, filled in some facts of marriage, a child, a new job in the extreme south and an address. Gail wrote from Madras, received a joyous tearful answer. Now we are on the bus from Kovilpatti to Kuzhithurai. At Tirunelveli and Nagercoil I change the packs from bus roof to bus roof and from my window seat observe the daily life of south India in the rice fields and village shops, bullock carts and diesel lorries, coconut palms and banana groves. Laundry is beat clean on stones around the shore of the village tank, then spread on the ground to dry in the blazing sun. Parmes teaches Tamil Literature at the small Women's College in Kuzhithurai. Can we break through conventions and customs to meet now freely as persons? Two diverse cultures also divide us.

On our first evening together we are free of traditional patterns allowing us to bridge some of this cultural diversity. Her husband, after work, has journeyed to their son's boarding school to bring him home the next day. We relax, eat leisurely in the cool twilight, like student friends, conversing softly, joining the threads of our separate lives together. The stars shine brightly over the small patio of their U-shaped house as we sit in the covered terrace forming the base of the U. The soft still light creates an atmosphere in which we soon feel joyful sympathy. Years of separation melt away for Gail and Parmes. I leave them conversing and slip under our mosquito net, soon asleep.

In the morning I begin to learn something of the structure and living patterns of her home. The kitchen is a dark room without a window, the red-tiled roof smoky black from the wood cooking fires in two pail-shaped clay fire pits on a raised platform above a concrete floor. Next to the kitchen is a grinding storage room containing a flat metate stone grinder and another with a cylindrical hole into which a large pestle fits. Both set on the dung-earth floor. Here rice is ground, heavy tedious labor, just as it was 2,000 years ago. Crocks of grains and spices line the walls. You begin a recipe from scratch. Across a small patio are three small rooms, one for trunk storage, another with a single bed having a crisscrossed rope bottom, surprisingly comfortable when covered by a quilt pad as a mattress and our mosquito net. A tiny alcove off the bedroom serves for daily family worship. Images of Siva and Parvati, fresh flowers, incense and candles are on the altar. A hall runs alongside these rooms with a cool tile floor on which Parames spreads a padded quilt for their bed, the coolest place to sleep in the house. Across the end of the patio connecting these two parts of the house is a porch with table and chairs, a pleasant place to sit, to eat or read or write or talk. At the opposite end of the patio a high wall joins the house walls, a water tap in the middle, the only tap in the house. At this tap in sunshine or moonlight you can bathe using a bucket or wash the dishes or clothes. In the far rear corner of the wall-enclosed yard is an outdoor toilet, merely a wall behind which you squat on the earth, cleaned once a day by the scavenger-sweeper. No plumbing, no heating, no sink, no stove, no refrigerator, no screens; no break-downs, no repairmen, no motors, no noise, no buttons to push. Perhaps it's better, who knows. That's all two incomes can afford. One lives and loves and enjoys. I like to bathe in the morning sunshine at the tap, the sky blue overhead, the wind in the banana trees or swaying the palms.

The local bus stops on a country road just outside Trivandrum, Kerala. I pass down our packs to Gail from the roof, we don them, and an Indian with whom we conversed on the bus leads us to the new home of Kuni and Laurie Baker, she a surgeon who special-izes in leprosy, he an architect creating low-cost buildings, friends of Gail's from the mountains of north India where they had built and operated a hospital in the Himalaya foothills. On the path below their unusual red brick buildings, Kuni meets us with warmth of spirit. Our small guest house, one of Laurie's ingenious designs, is a nest of curved walls, curved for strength because he builds of a single thickness of local brick, unplastered, using hollow tiles in the walls for structural reinforcing. Contrast this with the typical Indian house of thick poured concrete floors and walls using expensive steel rod reinforcing with ten or twenty times the needed strength. Laurie builds a home for one fourth or less the cost, but changing building styles is like trying to convince women not to use make-up. From their terraces on this hillside we look northeast across a valley of undulating cocunut palms to a ridge of mountains almost lost in haze. The kitchen-dining room is a separate structure of bamboo frame and thatch roof, the wall of long planks spaced and edged in a design that admits light and breeze. Whoever cooks is cool in this kitchen. To house four nieces from the country who wanted to go to schools and university in the city, Laurie quickly built a circular house of two floors and conical roof using a geometrical shape, the circle, that provides maximum space and strength. He used the same design on a massive scale to build a new cathedral in Tiruvella for Jacobite Christians. It was our pleasure to attend its dedication, dining with archbishops and seeing crowds of worshipers in festive dress. A band from a nearby Hindu temple played devotional music on traditional instruments, one a semicircular horn, a yard in diameter. Perhaps such a curve inspired another of Laurie's unusual designs, a home shaped like that horn whose interior space is a courtyard forming a dance platform for the woman who teaches dance. Room entrances face on to the inner court, and a second floor is accessible by an inner balcony. Windows face in and out. Structural strength comes from the curved red brick walls. The feeling of motion in this circular form is like a dancing *Nataraja* bronze.

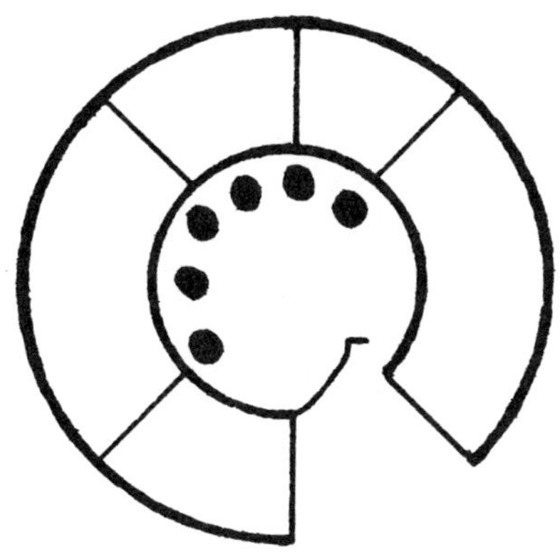

Most happily would I dwell here. India could adopt these

practical, inexpensive building techniques, brick and tile locally fired instead of cement and steel reinforcing rods, unplastered brick walls, conical roofs whose support is in the shape; yet India continues its British imitations.

Outside Trivandrum at Kovalam Beach on the Indian Ocean you can witness the invasion and oppression tourism brings to a coconut-palm beach glistening warm in winter. Jumbo jets fly in direct from Europe, air-conditioned buses ferry to the beach hotel or private thatch bungalow in the palms; a high wire fence topped with barbed strands and a guard at the gate keep Indians out. Laws prevent Indians from the enjoyment of their own beach. No beggars, no malnourished children, no lepers, no street-side shops; see nothing but clean white sand and then jumbo jet back again. Such vacation ghettos are springing up all over the world, alienated and alienating, artificial and artless, enriching and robbing, creating the One World of Tourists.

A unique landscape feature of Kerala are the coastal backwaters where you can travel for miles by small open ferry boats. We leave our bus at Alleppy, stroll to the dock for a long afternoon boat trip to Kottayam through lagoons and channels, a ferry for coconut plantation workers. In the brackish water floating plants blossom, violet carpets so thick the water is hidden, but our boat cuts through them as they softly slide by. Long narrow wooden canoe-shaped boats forty feet in length with artfully curved-up bow and stern are poled in the shallow water, carrying freight of all kinds — stone, sand, logs, dry goods and rice sacks — through a water land without roads. Silent and slim, they slide

through the floating gardens. Some have a tunnel-shaped roof of woven coconut palms. Small wooden canoes carry farmers to their rice fields below water level drained by diesel pumps that gush the water into the canals. When were these stone embankments made? So many ways have been invented to make water useful, from water mill to electric dynamo, from dike to irrigation channel, for bathing, drinking, cooking. Water is full of meaning for human existing. Place a vase of water on your altar.

The British built hill stations for cool summer capitals away from the tropical heat of the plains, at Ootacamund even a race track. It is a beautiful setting in a high valley, and there is a romantic pleasure if you come up in the narrow-gauge, cog-wheel train. You alight and breathe deep the cool, fresh air. Above the station is the Das Prakash belonging to an Indian hotel chain known for its fine vegetarian food, offering a grand vista over the town and valley. We enjoy the arrangement of the dining room. Guests sit on the outside of a U-shaped marble-top table while waiters serve from inside the U, carrying their bowls and pots in a rhythm through the double swinging doors. It's easy to converse with a stranger facing you on the opposite side, in winter wrapped in a blanket, a scarf around his head, his newlywed wife clad in a fine Kashmir shawl. The couples seem to come in foursomes, helping each other to get acquainted in an arranged marriage.

For a day's outing we take the local bus over the ridge to the village of Nanjanad, the end of the route, scan the surrounding hills and pick our ramble. On the village street, various grains and pulses are sun-drying: ragi, oats, rice, beans. We savor the fragrance of the Eucalyptus groves, often grown to shade the tea bushes, and sit vista gazing, reading aloud from Stuart Piggott's *Some Ancient Cities of India* about places we will visit as we make our way north.

Of the many beautiful temples throughout India, one of the loveliest in every respect is Somnathpur, southeast of Mysore. Every minute detail unites in an overall architectural harmony. You enter the rectangular courtyard by mounting several steps to the small platform in the gate and so frame your visual contemplation. On the inside of the courtyard wall small cells face an open corridor supported by columns that may seem squat or fat at first, but their profiles arrest your eyes in a rhythm of horizontal layers, each column slightly varying the pulse. The overall floor plan of the temple is a cross whose transepts and apse are slightly more than half

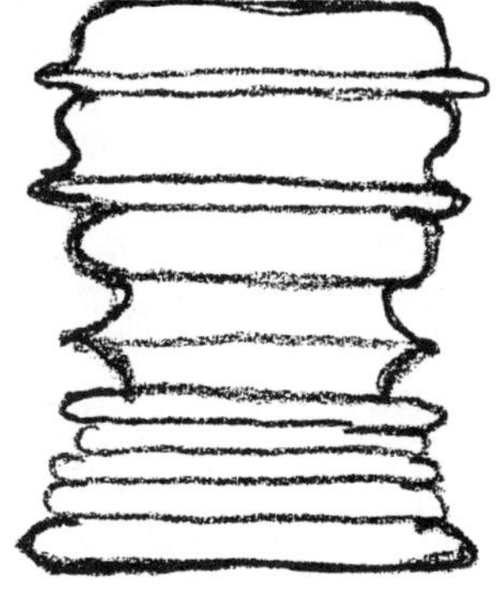

of a sixteen-pointed star surmounted by towers that are sixteen-sided star cones. The long leg of the cross contains an entrance hall to the square chamber of the gods. The building is raised four feet above a paved courtyard on a ten-layered stone base, five alternate layers recessed, that gives a floating feeling to the platform. My dimensions and sketches are not accurate. I carry no instruments. I want the feel of the building, how my vision senses it.

The ambulatory around the temple conforms to the shape of the walls while the walls at eye level consist of six parallel bands, each slightly less in height than the one below, in a richly-carved frieze. Starting at the bottom is a parade of elephants, tusk touching tail; second, a cavalry armed with spears. In the third level, a floral pattern of reversing 'S' curves ends at the corners in a Kala face. Next we see the *Ramayana* stories in stone, full of naturalistic human, animal and even divine forms, an imaginative plethora of creativity. But the world is fierce and fearful so we have a frieze of monsters whose bodies are half lion, half boar, their faces carved to scare you, glaring eyes, snorting nostrils, rippling muscles. At the top we return to peace again with a parade of geese in their stately gait, not a hiss to be heard. Each parade shows some misbehaving animals who turn around and face the rear just when you don't expect it.

To educate all newly-married couples you'll find loving scenes in the entrance hall on the south wall in the top band, seven panels measuring six by eight inches. Most Indian temples have these panels. I like to find them. From east to west are: two lovers standing, her leg up over his hip in this classic Indian pose; he seated on a bench, she on the floor, turning her head to take him in; she stands braiding the hair of a young girl, he enters her from behind; both on a bed, she beneath, he licking her, she sucking him with wonderful naturalistic rhythms; both standing, arm in arm facing you, smiling; a repeat of the second panel; both on a bed, she half reclined beneath, legs raised high, firmly joined together, arms around each other, playfully kissing and moving. Days with these sculptures can liberate. Today many Indians refuse to look. Perhaps in ancient times a healthy frankness and sensuous joy gave a spirit of playfulness and celebration to this creativity.

In the transepts and apse under the three towers are three chambers, each with its deity. The ceilings are large floral displays forming royal umbrellas whose centers are beautiful banana buds. Above the six-level frieze four-foot high male and female deities are arranged in pairs, males on each side of the star-points, females on each side of the recesses, of the sixteen-pointed towers, powerfully realistic and sensuously delightful. I wonder if the sixteen-pointed stars are the compass points: N, NNE, NE, ENE, E, ESE, SE, SSE, S, SSW, SW, WSW, W, WNW, NW, NNW. The temple faces east. What astronomical meanings are embodied? Amidst these star-shaped towers took up to a firmament of floating stars.

In the small town of Belur we find all the restaurants closed because of a student strike against inflationary prices. Tired and hungry after an all-day bus ride, we dip into emergency rations from our packs: dried fruits, nuts, powdered milk and cereals. Once more we are pleased with our planning — what we need when we need it. Sleep. Emergency food for breakfast. Renewed energy. We're off to see Belur Temple, an architectural design similar to Somnathpur but not so well realized except for a series of dancers and musicians around the top of the wall tilted forty-five degrees over you, free-standing, showing a great delicacy and mastery of carving, exquisite in texture and form, graceful and alive. We sit for some time gazing at each one, talking about their figures and the day slips by. Worshipers and tourists walk by quickly, staring at us or clicking their cameras. I wonder repeatedly how I can teach people to stop, rest, sit, look, talk, look some more, enjoy. Can there be no leisure in their lives?

Halebid Temple enjoys a lovely location beside a small lake, fall colors in the trees reflecting in the water. Conveniently adjacent is the Inspection Bungalow where our porch overlooks the profusely-carved temple. Each hour of the day changes the shadows of the deep relief and highlights different features. We walk around at midday, sunset, dawn, mid-morning, mid-afternoon. The groundplan is complex, suggesting two periods of construction. Originally, I suspect, there were two buildings, each in the form of a compound Greek cross. These were connected by a hallway. On the east side, opposite each, are two small rectangular temples without walls, roofs supported by eighteen columns. Under one is a large *Nandi* (bull), sacred beast to Hindus. Sit on the bench in the cool breeze off the lake: *Nandi* will keep you quiet company. On the west side, opposite the two separate temples, one section of the compound Greek cross is replaced by an eight-pointed semi-circle, the sixteen-pointed circular design of Somnathpur, but the symmetry is broken by a small rectangular projection at the north and south points. So the entire building is asymmetrical in its longitudinal halves from an aerial view, but since you can rarely see both sides at once in your circumambulation, this asymmetry turns into a delightful variety. The relief frieze on the east side resembles that of Somnathpur but has two additional bands. In one dancers alternate with geese, in the other floral designs separate lion-boar monsters. Imagine a dancer moving gracefully among the stately geese. On the west side you'll find five-foot figures of gods and goddesses, scantily or elaborately dressed in ribboned drapery, necklaces and high crowns or coiffures of hair, all their anatomy subtly accented by the ribboned drapery.

One kilometer south of Halebid Hindu Temple lies the Jain temple of Basthi, a spatial proximity we have encountered before. Jainism was born alongside Buddhism, Mahavira and Gautama both seeking to reform Hinduism at the time of Socrates and Confucius. In this Jain temple stands a twenty-foot Mahavira figure, blissful and powerful, captivating and serene, in his nudity representing the highest humanity, not needing any material possessions or adornments. These statues, always in the same simple standing posture, have a strange power that I cannot attribute to any unusual features of the carving. Perhaps that is the secret — a man stands simply before you, devoid of anything beyond himself, sufficient unto himself. Let a person be just what he or she is, without possessions, material or psychological, and you already have Nietzsche's overman, a transcendental being who is utterly free of dependence on this world and therefore wholly in this world. The purity of Jainism has not made it a popular religion, but it is a deeply moving one for those who yearn for pure being. Let no being molest another being in the slightest way: sweep clean your path.

To hear Krishna play his flute we walk half a mile east of Basthi to the small temple of Kethareswara. In the rectangular entrance hall Krishna plays, every finger in his hands deftly carved, poised over the flute holes, just as we heard the music in the temple at Annamalai. The far end of the entrance hall opens into a semi-circular vaulted eight-pointed star, half the typical sixteen-pointed star, a building design of great simplicity and charm. The motif and meaning of this sixteen-pointed star fascinate me. I would gladly come each morning with the dawn to hear him play.

Bouncing along all day in the bus again, Halebid to Arrikere to Hubli, 8 a.m. to 7 p.m., through New Mexico-like semi-desert, our home country, my ears plugged with kleenex wads against the engine noise, a long silent way to the Brinavan Hotel in Hubli. Shower, supper, sleep. We awaken to street noises, vendors call, carts clatter on the pock-marked pavement, taxi horns blare for right of way. I stand on our balcony eating bread and oranges, sipping coffee, absorbing the activity below. The joy of a hot-water shower, a second breakfast at midmorning near the bus station, omelettes and coffee. On the outskirts of Badami the driver drops us in front of the dak bungalow. We arrange for a room, order supper, hang our mosquito net, spread our bag-sheet, undress, stretch out to rest while the heat of midday abates. Late afternoon we walk into town, espy one of the temple-caves from the road junction, take our bearings and plunge into a maze of narrow streets, children practicing their school-English, "What's your name?" "What is your native place?" We emerge from the maze and climb the hill to the first rock-cut temple.

At the tops of the sixth-century square coloumns are circular medallions picturing affectionate couples in the joy of loving, touching, kissing, laughing. These medallions show another facet of Hindu culture's celebration of life. Sitting on a flat railing, I hear the rhythmic slap-slap of women washing clothes on the shore of the lake below. A flat stone worn smooth from slapping precedes the mechanical agitation of a washing machine. The rhythmic slapping produces a reverie that transports me back thousands of years to when those flat stones were first laid on the lake shore, not yet worn, a very sturdy machine. The third temple crowns our afternoon of aesthetic joy with reliefs on a majestic scale at the ends of the first colonnade. The stone flesh of the gods is alive here. On the top half of the front column we find life-size couples arm in arm, faces turned towards each other in tender smiles, blessing you to take this way of life, the way of pure mutual affection between lovers. I sit on the floor in dazed contemplation. No where else in the world is affection so displayed. It is as pure as the Madonna and Child. I feel the same affection for philosophical ideas, each full of tenderness towards me, waiting patiently for my understanding, telling me there is no need to choose one as superior, but to be a lover of each, nursed by their inner spirit, graced by their subtle charms, enlightened by their smiling meanings. These couples speak to me.

> Badami caves are wondrous
> Temples carved into a cliff.
> Sculptured gods and loving couples,
> Arms entwined in pure affection,
> Adorn square columns and walls.
> Circular vault in the ceiling
> Moulded of a coiled cobra
> Sheltering a god in its hood.

Part way down we climb out onto a boulder on the face of the cliff to watch the sunset and are surprised to find two monkeys already seated to watch the sunset. They've been studying those affectionate temple carvings, for they sit, one holding the other encircled in his arms. We sit like them as the colors form and fade. He carefully goes over her shoulders, back, arms, parting the hair looking for annoying insects. She turns her face round to his kissing and hugging, full of affection, students of Hindu sculpture.

Where else in the world do you see so much affection given to the slow powerful obedient water buffalo and bullock, see them daily bathed and carefully scrubbed in some muddy tank; even their long curled horns are shined and painted. Often at evening we watch them bathed after a long day plowing rice paddies or trudging along a dusty road. These beasts manifest the perfect detached deliberateness characteristic of an enlightened sage. No wonder Hindus have come to venerate the bullock with his great hump of wisdom that bears against the yoke. Nandi bull becomes an animal manifestation of the god carved in vivid naturalness at many Hindu temples. Children love to climb on his neck for a placid ride.

Twenty kilometers from Badami lies Pattadakal, where you see both North and South Indian temple styles side by side in purity of form. The Northern style has a hyberbolic tower mounted on a cube base while the Southern or Dravidian is a pyramid of flattened cubes. Both kinds have a rectangular entrance hall usually facing east. Out of these basic geometrics architects wrought many variations, some so far removed as to defy stylistic relation. At Pattadakal, one temple in the Northern style adds a hallway around the cube made of huge flat slabs for ceiling and walls, while one in the Southern style has a fascinating assortment of different stone lattice-work designs for its windows.

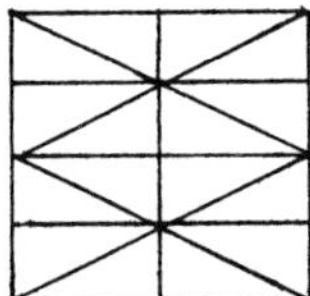 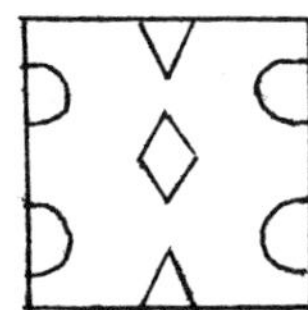 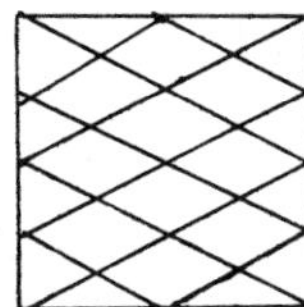 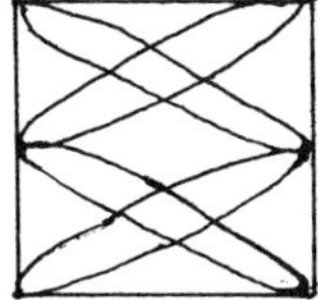

(My ink lines are the stone ribs while the white is space.)

Pattadakal
Essences of Indian Architecture
Standing side by side.
Dravidian cubes of descending size
Elongated dome, a giant lingam.
An entrance hall facing east takes you in.
Green parrots flit from each to each
Chattering mantras for Chalukyan kings.

Clickity click over the many miles, our train from Badami to Ellora passes towns and villages whose names are fascinating sounds. On the parched earth labor crews of peasants — women, men and children — work at building roads, breaking rock with sledge hammers, moving earth in head baskets, leveling grades by hand shovels, employed by the government in exchange for food because of long drought. Thin adults, pot-bellied children despoiled by the barren land. Who is the Hindu god of rain?

On the railroad from Badami
Guludgud road, a highway crossing
Bagalkot where a cement plant pollutes
Kadlimatti and Sitimani

Basavana and Bagewadi
Dryer and dryer grows the land
Five years without good monsoon rains
Earth cracked and parched at Mulvad
Honaganahilli and Minchmal.

Ellora — a continuous cliff of hard sandstone in a river gorge; a mecca of rock-carved temples, Buddhist, Hindu, Jain. It is a place for pilgrimage, a place with power to heal and inspire. Most of the temples are cut into the cliff yielding an architecture of interior space but having no exterior form, great halls of columns, relief panels and free-standing sculptures. In a strange way, one enjoys the full religious and artistic use of the temple without a need for exterior walls or roof, an enormous saving of labor. By contrast, the Kailasa temple possesses its exterior architecture, the entire cliff cut down in a grand monolith whose ground size equals the Parthenon and whose height is one and a half times as great. It is the most majestic of rock-cut temples, beautifully carved everywhere, an aesthetic-spiritual unity expressing a high point of Indian civilization, under the monarch Krishna I (757-783 A.D.). Our delight is unbounded. We dream of living nearby. Time melts to nothing.

On the second day I discover the third floor of number twelve, Tinthal, a Buddhist temple. Here I spend an entire afternoon until sunset when the horizontal rays penetrate to the rear of the hall, illuminating one panel after another. I judge that on the Spring and Fall Equinox the sun will shine on the central Buddha. You could easily miss Tinthal because the first floor is unfinished but remember that a rock temple is carved from the top down so the earliest and complete work is to be found on the top floor contrary to your normal expectations. When you walk down the center aisle of the top floor toward the fine Buddha enshrined in the rear wall, you can turn your head to either side looking down the six side aisles past four square columns to a deep relief panel, each a masterpiece of composition and carving. Each panel has a Buddha in full-lotus position or with legs down. The variations come in the attendant figures. The geometrical alignment of the tapered columns set off the overall proportions of the room. On the rear wall on each side of the central shrine are panels of seven male Buddhas while both side walls within the shrine chamber have

three female Buddhas with Gautama in the center. Low-relief
floral panels throughout are a botanical paradise.

Third floor — Tinthal — Ellora
Memories of Java and Japan
Buddhas — male and female
Full lotus or legs down.

Walk down the center aisle
Gautama framed in the columns
Side aisles ending in deep relief
Forty-two square pillars perfectly aligned.

Ajanta — a great sweeping bend in the river exposes hard
sandstone cliffs for temple-caves, once a fresco painter's
paradise, now faded by dampness and smoke-black. Temple
seventeen still has some brilliant colors and sharp outlines. Faces
are of every color: green, red, black, white, brown. Was it not
Matisse who shocked Paris with a green face? Ajanta painters did
it long ago. Look, too, at how a single line draws an entire face or
body. Did Picasso study here? Temple eleven displays a vestibule
ceiling with abstract cubist designs, literally arranging and
unfolding a cube in two dimensions long before modern Cubism
arose in Europe. Ajanta reveals a fantastic range of composition
from representational to symbolic and abstract, from landscape to
portraiture, from floral designs to still life. Where are these
painters in present-day India? What happened to this creative
power? These paintings are not restricted to a framed canvas but
decorate walls and ceiling in a compositional unity, side aisle set
off by a row of columns of great variety. The small Buddhist stupa
in the apse reminds me of a small medieval chapel. Strange that
the solid arch was not transferred to free-standing stone block
construction.

To gain maximum daylight inside some temples we have to
plan our visit according to the sun's position. Now that Ajanta is a
tourist attraction with gates open only from nine till four, you
cannot catch the sunrise and sunset illuminations that I'm certain
were planned for some temples, for instance temple twenty-six for
sunrise. We arrive as early as we can after several days of
exploring, calculating and planning our visit. Around the walls are
deep-relief panels beginning on your left with a reclining Buddha
reminiscent of the large outdoor reclining Buddha at Polonnaruva

in Sri Lanka. This pose conveys a simple, direct message: Buddha
rests and sleeps and converses at leisure, relaxed and enjoying
repose. Here is a wisdom not to be neglected. Buddha is seen
not judging, not preaching, not creating, not protecting, not
aiding — just resting. In the next panel we encounter one of the
sculptural wonders of our journey, a composition of curves and
triangles formed by the rhythm of fifteen young women below a
seated Buddha with a battle scene above or behind him. We feel it
is a temptation scene in which Buddha is neither allured by the
women nor disturbed by the battle, unattached, understanding
both. I give the spatial arrangement of the heads, for your eyes
travel from one face to another, back and forth and around,
forming a pattern of triangles and curves. I feel the movement as I
contemplate its rhythm. With a shift of key my eyes travel in

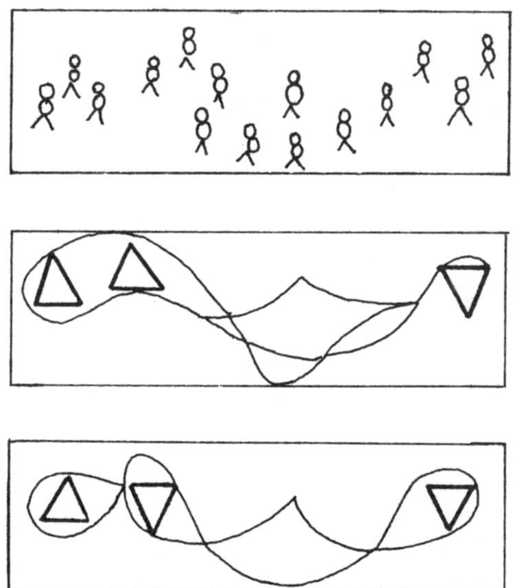

another set of curves. I sit in total rapture, sensing the motion of
the curves, alive to the beauty of these figures. The triangular
spaces serve to anchor the shifting patterns of curves, providing
stability to the highly charged energy in the curves.

We ask the attendant guard to open the windows so as to gain
more illumination but he says it's against the rules. Later in
temple seven, the attendant has opened the windows and

constructed a reflecting board from the unfolded tinfoil of cigarette packages laid side by side on a four-foot square board which he holds in the sun, reflecting its rays on the sculptures you wish to see. His compassion reveals someone far along the karmic path toward eventual release and nirvana. He aids you like the ferryman in Buddhist mythology.

At temple twenty-six, we delight in the two side doorways with their borders of pairs of standing lovers, some seated on top, in affectionate poses with an especially handsome dancer at the bottom of each side border. Buddhism celebrates human affection as one expression of its infinite compassion. Simple pilgrims see for themselves ways of living to imitate.

This affection gains bold expression in a surprising way in temple twenty where lesbian couples at the tops of the entrance columns tilt over you as at Halebid. The taller woman has her arm around the neck of the smaller woman, her hand on her breast. Inside, the same pose is carved for all worshipers to easily see; so frank, so powerful, so gracious. Buddhist art has transcended a persistent patriarchial oppression. We are deeply moved by these sculptures with their strong affirmation.

We take our lunch of rice, *dhal*, vegetable *bidiani*, chapatis, coffee, at the archeological canteen, chatting with a social anthropologist from Cambridge who lives at the Forest Rest House where we are staying. I try to express to him my ideas about the metaphysics of archeology. What is it that draws me, a philosopher, to seek out archeological sites and try to feel their spirit in architecture, sculpture, painting, setting? Metaphysicians seek to understand and describe the contours of the Universe, the most abstract and fundamental principles and entities of reality, of being-as-such. Religions embody a perspective of this Reality felt with visionary inspiration for the pursuit of a way of life. To convey its way of life to people, a religion seeks an expression of its way in visible and audible forms of architecture, sculpture, painting, dance, literature and music. The archeological metaphysician seeks a route to Reality by way of re-experiencing these artistic expressions of a religion in its temples. That is why I sit in contemplation of temples — Buddhist, Hindu, Jain, Islamic.

If you like the portrait style of El Greco, you can see the work of his earlier incarnation in temple nine where on your left stand six bodhisattvas done in gold and dark colors whose faces especially remind me of El Greco's work. Ajanta has brought home to me the universality of styles of painting. If we only possessed a range of canvases from Greek civilization we could test this universality in a more familiar culture. On one of your last days in Ajanta, visit temple twelve where you can select one of the twelve rooms, each with two stone bunks or benches, no paintings, no carvings, but offering a vista out across the river canyon focused by the temple entrance, an aesthetic achieved by framing a view; recline, focus, concentrate, undistracted by your vision.

At the railway station in Jalgon I become deeply depressed by one extreme of India: dust, grime, rubbish, spitting, pissing, coughing, sneezing, beggars with miserable sores and filaria victims with monstrous limbs. India is not an easy country to travel in. I'm haunted by a fear of disease. I exercise great care with all food, drink, contact with insects and people. Gandhi made a life-long effort to influence his people, to change their habits. He admonished them not to spit, to cover their shit with soil for manure, to cover their wells. He knew how crucial to the general health these practices were. He failed utterly not only to alter these living patterns but also to create a non-violent, non-industrial, non-possessive India. This side of India wears me down.

We change trains in Itarsi and stop for the night in a Railway Retiring Room in Bhopal; clean, comfortable, with hot water for a change. Bathe at midnight and lie close on the single bed, all that was available, talking and caressing.

> A loving couple
> Sleeping in a single bed
> Washed and lying skin to skin
> Gently touching everywhere
> Arms enfolding one another
> Noses tip to tip
> Turning in our sleep together

Sometimes when we are in the midst of a beautiful temple we wonder about the living and working conditions of those who labored to build them. Imagine the fine rock dust from the carving within the narrow confines of cave-temples, no fans to bring in fresh air, lungs slowly filling with dust till they weaken, collapse and die. Is great art worth these human lives? Weren't the American Indians far better off not erecting such stone temples, roaming free the plains and woods, breathing clean air, their possessions few, living in harmony with the land, enjoying fresh water, fish, meat, nuts, corn, squash. They created a culture without cities. Doesn't the passion to create permanent temples really enslave human beings? What does it matter if we have no archeological remains of the nomadic Indians? Isn't a life in harmony with the coming-to-be and passing-away of nature wiser than the passion for immortality in stone?

From a long way off you can see the Great Stupa of Sanchi, framed against the blue sky, on the hilltop rising in the midst of a broad flat valley, fields of green wheat stretching away on all sides. This distant perspective of the stupa provides impressions that gradually take on meaning for me. After siesta I combine them with close-up views gathered in the late afternoon. In the twilight we descend, treading worn stone steps of Buddhist pilgrims, feeling joy and calm. After supper my reflections play with the meanings of these forms.

The great hemispherical shape of a Buddhist stupa — what is the meaning of this form? Is it the great dome of the sky, blue by day and star-speckled at night, that shelters us? Is it the pregnant belly about to give birth or the rounded breast that nurses us? Is it the geometrical form, without distinction on its surface, on which no one point is more important, distinctive, attractive than another, a non-attachment to any one point? Is it the ever-present hill the pilgrim must climb in hope of liberation, the sacred mountain, the height of wisdom to be realized? Is it not the very form or half-form of the cosmos, of planets and stellar bodies? Is it the shape of the eye, a wisdom eye in the middle of your brow? Suppose your religion believes there should be no images of its founder, no temples erected, then what shape could you use for a memorial? A hemisphere. So the Buddhists constructed stupas until in the long course of time they could no longer resist those powerful anthropomorphic forces in us and carved the Buddha's image seated in meditation, and on his head they often placed a hemispheric crown of snails. How long and patiently you must sit in meditation for the slow snails to crawl up your body to gather in a crown on your head.

In the early morning we climb the pilgrim steps to the smaller
Stupa Two. On each of the broad flat stone posts of the fence
around the stupa are carved three low-relief medallions, a circular
one in the middle and two semicircular ones above and below.
Among the great variety of floral and geometrical patterns are
animals, birds and people. As the sun changes its position we
move in order to catch the shadow etching that brings out the form
of each design. Later in the week we return at other times of the
day to extend our shadow design discoveries.

> Halfway up the hillside
> Stupa Two awaits you
> Surrounded by a strange fence
> Tall, flat, serene stone rails
> Set in square stone pillars.
> Three medallions sculptured
> Half circles top and foot
> Floral geometrics
> Playful animal scenes.
> Circumambulations
> Satisfy our senses.

Another morning we meditate visually on the gates of the
Great Stupa with their triple lintels and superb carving standing
so free and clear yet solidly placed. Between lookings I read
Aurobindo's *The Significance of Indian Art,* a sensitive appre-
ciation. Yet I feel he plays down the sensuous-sexual for the
spiritual, a common human failing. I look up from my reading to
see hawks catching an updraft over the stupa, bound on their way.

> Hawks on the hunt
> Catching an updraft over the stupa
> Gliding graceful above Sanchi
> Eyeing the ground for prey.
>
> Apul's search for meaning
> Through the gates of Sanchi
> Stepping softly to the terrace
> Vision wandering upward.

These Sanchi gates remind me of the Shinto *tori* gates of Japan,
free-standing, with several lintels. Sometimes I've wondered if
one hour a day of *zazen* is enough. Reading Aurobindo makes
clear to me that I was doing *zazen* all day long in Japan, looking at

scrolls, sensing flower arrangements, pondering rock gardens, talking with Ogata, sliding open my rice-paper panels on the garden.

Some days have exactly the right combination of ingredients, an aesthetic whole in the art of living. We rented bicycles, had lunch packed, pedaled away between the wheat fields beneath the shade of a tree-lined road, bound for Vidisha and then to Udaigiri Caves. The pace of a bicycle suits human vision, clear views all around by turning your head, effortless on the level. We enjoy the same pace while canoeing on a lake. Riding side by side, we converse easily, sometimes holding hands. Few cars disturb us, we pass bullock carts at their snail's pace. On a bridge we stop to watch the morning laundry, colorful saris spread on the sand to dry, bodies glistening after their bath. A side road takes us to Udaigiri cave-temples where surprising forms await us. Cave-temple four has a lingam with a human head carved on one side in full relief, fine loose hair and full round face. I saw no lingam like this in the South. The standing figures on each side of the doorway of cave-temple six have a wonderful fidelity in their stomach muscles. In cave five the massive Vishnu-boar, attended by a gracious earth goddess, manifests a powerful incarnation of spirit. To the right are rows of standing figures, one row of men with long pointed beards, dressed in Scotch-like kilts. Who are they? Professor Davidson tells me at supper that they puzzle him too. In the background an ocean shore bordered by a profusion of lotus blossoms and buds reminds me of Monet's ''Water Lilies.'' There is an exquisitely carved garland around Vishnu's neck.

In this remote countryside are cave-temple carvings of superb quality. What a testimonial to the pervasive spiritual power of a civilization. Few civilizations achieve this power. Think of people whose lives are so tuned to the spiritual and artistic as to blossom in this way. Here the philosopher encounters a profound wisdom.

Another morning at Sanchi, I return to ponder the small carvings of affectionate couples around the base of the entrance of the Hindu-like temple east of the Great Stupa. They are choice postures that inspire me.

> Hip to hip
> An arm around each other's shoulders
> Half-turned faces smile in joy.

A hand curves softly to the thigh.
One leg crossed behind the other
Rests deftly on the toes.
Two affectionate lovers stand
Her foot gently rests on his.

At sunset the green swallows return from the fields, gliding over and around the Great Stupa before roosting in one tree on the southeast. They remind me of the swallows returning at sunset to the Mayan temple of Sayil in Yucatán. Swallows love all temples.

Building in stone is not easily altered. Architects must dare to combine contrasting forms, not knowing for sure the aesthetic outcome. While at Sanchi you can test such an adventure by looking at different times at the square fence that surrounds the triple umbrella on top of the Great Stupa. I find the square fence too strong a contrast with the hemispherical dome, a clash of forms without a harmonizing union. In conjunction with the rectangularity of the gates, it almost succeeds but they stand too far apart. An architectural dare that does succeed for me is the design of the columns in the ruined temple south of the Great Stupa. At three fourths of its height each square column has notches cut into it, accented in the stone by a new moon crescent above and below. The vertical feeling of the column is not destroyed as you might expect. Appreciating these experiments requires aesthetic time, a time that is broken into separate viewings, a cyclic time of returnings, intervals of absence for reflective reveries, a sun time of shadow changes. Hence the aesthetic traveler's axiom: stay awhile, don't rush on.

Another traveler's axiom is flexibility: make no reservations far ahead. Packed and ready for the afternoon train, we return from our morning at the Stupa. Parked out front is a Landrover, that special English vehicle unrivaled for rugged terrain, piloted by a Dutch couple. Over lunch we discover many sympathetic points of view with Hans and Hanneke van Riel, school teachers. We change our plans, stay another night and ride with them to Khajuraho, enjoying fine conversation over the next few days.

North Indian Hindu temples achieve their classic perfection at Khajuraho (950-1050 A.D.). Their towers embody a skyward thrust in which I feel the movement of each individual human self, *atman*, toward identity with the absolute, *brahma*. In the horizontal friezes, usually two or three bands, around the temples, the carving is sensuous and vital, humorous and graceful, often depicting the powerful energy of sexual creativity. These horizontal bands depict the multitudinous and inexhaustible force of creating by Vishnu who is one manifestation of the absolute. The figures are sculptured in high relief about half life size. Visitors, unfortunately, often see these figures as erotic, and tourism has played upon this aspect, but there is no doubt in my mind that we are witnessing here a deep religious expression of the vital fecundity and sweeping inclusiveness of these two central tenants of Hinduism. I can think of no more appropriate way to present dramatically these abstract philosophic-religious ideas in an understandable form to worshipers. Khajuraho allows us to return in time to a civilized peak of morally uninhibited human expression of the highest spiritual quality.

Away from the main temple area, southeast across the wheat fields, are the exquisite temples of Vamana, Javari and Duladeo. How I love to wander free for the whole day to these temples. Insects, flowers, birds and clouds create an atmosphere that fills me with joy. I see a mound covered with weeds, grass, shrubs. My fancy imagines a temple once standing there. I turn aside to tramp over it and in the tangled weeds I find a complete capital of a column, carved with naga figure, unbroken, a treasure left in the weeds. Every mound now captivates me and several reveal broken carvings. What would excavations turn up?

At Vamana Temple on all the corners are the most graceful women in India, sometimes placed on two sides of a concave corner, often facing each other, clearly couples, tall, slim, alluring profiles, bewitching smiles, eyes alive. I sit.for hours on several days wholly captivated by these sculptured women. I bring my book to read by them, Bachelard's *Poetics of Reverie*, or my journal to write in.

> Vamana Temple, eastern group, Khajuraho
> Pairs of tall, slim, graceful women
> Placed to face each other on inner corners —
> Deep navel on soft tummy
> Plucking a thorn out of her foot
> Holding her breast in cupped hand
> Scratching the middle of her back

Shyly with a hand over half her face
Stretching her torso with arm behind head
Searching her face in a mirror
One hip thrust out in joy

At Javari Temple, two hundred yards south, I meet these graceful pairs once more. The whole long morning disappears in aesthetic rapture. The entrance halls contain a wealth of carving housed in rooms of perfect proportion. Before the sun-heat is too intense I saunter slowly along the farmer's narrow paths, across his fields to the Temple of Duladeo. The circular dome ceiling of the entrance hall with its hanging banana bud in the center is the finest I can recall. Passing no village market on the way, our lunch is only bread and water. Shirts off, we sun-bathe and nap on the flat slabs of the terrace. The twenty apsara figures listed in the 1971 guide are missing from the entrance hall. Stolen art treasures? One night during our stay at Sanchi, a four-foot free-standing female figure was stolen from the north gate lintel. India pilfered; a crime against art, the triumph of money.

Spread over the fields, at intervals of a hundred yards, are wells yielding water, jug by jug. Teams of bullocks walk round and round turning the creaking wooden gears. Clay jugs tied to a rope that moves down into the well scoop up water and dump it into a wooden trough leading to the fields. A man walks round behind the bullocks, prodding them on all day. When will the diesel pump invade?

Khajuraho has become the erotic sculpture paradise of the world, an unfortunate misunderstanding. Indian Air Lines flies tourists in each morning, takes them on a guided tour to see the spectaculars, flies them out in the afternoon. We siesta between eleven and two while their cameras click; they haven't time to stay overnight so we wait until they are gone. Each tourist season the crowds increase. We are thankful for a little peace before the conquest of world tourism is complete. New forms of swift travel crisscross the world carrying tourists from one identical international hotel to the next.

By bus and train we journey from Khajuraho to Bubaneswara, breaking our trip in Calcutta to enjoy a long afternoon in the Calcutta Museum. One room contains the fence and gate from the Buddhist Stupa of Bharhut, providing me a rhythmic balance of

Sanchi, Khajuraho, Bharhut and Bhubaneswara. I spend most of the afternoon in contemplation of the sculpture of fence and gate: fresh, alive, vigorous, life-size, male and female, feet turned out 180°. There is an exceptional standing Buddha from Muthura; another piece from Bodh Gaya shows a loving couple in a position Gail and I have nicknamed Buddha's bride — he sits in half-lotus position with her in his lap face to face.

Bhubaneswara is another paradise for temple lovers. Some thirty temples, large and small, spanning five centuries, 750-1250 A.D., are scattered through the town. I bubble with excitement to see them again after an interval of fifteen years. Beginning at Parameswara, a museum piece for this style, we are captivated by the two lattice or perforated stone windows on each side of the west doorway whose 'grill' or 'ribs' are beautifully carved, dancers and musicians with trumpet, lute and symbol. At Mukteswara, the overall harmony of delicate carving culminates in the archway in front of the entrance whose carver possessed consumate skill. Rajarani Temple, dating from the third and latest period, manifests a refinement of curves and contours of a well-developed style. Its carved figures are set off by exquisite geometric filagree.

Another morning we engage a bicycle ricksaw to ride out to Brahmeswara Temple whose form, carving and setting attract us. We linger for the entire morning, our aesthetic senses respond, we feel the beautiful pouring into our consciousing; here is an aesthetic of existing. Slowly we circumambulate, climb up onto the wall to walk around at a higher level, sit for long ponderings at different perspectives. We know at once that we will return for sunset. We recognize intuitively that this is a place for us. How does this happen? What synthetic act of consciousing unites aesthetic components with features of our existing in a totality so positive? There is an interdependence, a reciprocity, an interaction in which psychological or conscious forms of our feelings respond to the sculptural forms of the figures, for instance, a recognition of identical forms of sensuousness, physical and conscious. There is a transaction between the spatial forms of the artistic object and the conscious forms of our psychic feelings. Unless these conscious forms are present, aesthetic experience cannot transpire.

When we return before sunset I fall in love with one figure at Rajarani Temple near Brahmeswara. Carved in red sandstone, the setting sun intensifies her color. She stands on the west side, lower row, the first figure to the north of the empty center niche. The soft texture of the stone, her subtle smile, the graceful curve of her torso, her left leg bent at the knee, the proportions of her body, all express a psychic power that enfolds me as the brilliant glow fades into the twilight of evening, gradually enfolding her. She waits there patiently to greet you.

Begin or end your temple journey in India at Konarak or Mamallapuram, sea temples on the shore of the great Bay of Bengal. We end at Konarak, the Sun Temple dedicated to Surya, the sun-god, a wonder of sculptural delights, boasting a variety of *naga* (snake-human) figures, and gods carved in a smooth polished chlorite of a blue-green-black color. Before us are days of aesthetic pleasure absorbing the sensuous grace and joy of this celebration of creative vitality, a tantric mecca. Day after day, around and around we amble, delighted with the lovely embodiments of male and female hips and hands, arms and ankles, torsos and thighs. Nothing is left out, all is shown, to evoke the aesthetic identity of carved form and psychic feeling that produces aesthetic experience. Our eyes enjoy these forms while our reflections comprehend their expression of the creative inclusiveness of Hinduism. In this historical period Hinduism achieved a pinnacle of balance between an early phase groping for an appropriate artistic and ritualistic portrayal of the ideals of ceaseless creativity and complete containment of every possible existent thing, and a later phase of rigid moralistic prescriptions aimed at sheer preservation of a past no longer understood. We look at these lovers caressing each other, legs and arms artfully entwined, sucking, licking, fingering, smiles of orgasmic climax, singly, in pairs and triples with occasional playful sexual jokes that make us laugh from surprise. Some feel shock, not joyful surprise leading to understanding. To appreciate Konarak, transcend moral taboos, break through barriers of religious repression to a liberation fully human. We feel Konarak achieves a marvelous artistic statement of cosmic creativity in human lovers.

One morning at Konarak I sit long in two places: on the top of

the eastern-most wheel on the south side gazing at the east facade
illuminated in the morning sun and on the platform of horses on
the south side, leaning against the base in the cool shade of late
morning. I contemplate one large amorous sculpture in a deep
niche. Many pilgrims have arrived today for their annual cele-
bration of the sun-god's power. Konarak comes alive. Simple
Indian peasants circumambulate, smiling, wondering, under-
standing.

> Three on a pedestal
> Within a recessed niche
> Fine amorous triade —
> He caressing her cheek
> Her leg over his hip
> Between their legs the third
> Her head tilted backwards
> Lovingly sucks and licks.
> Southeast-east Konarak.
>
> Deep within a corner
> Stands an amorous pair —
> His hand upon her hip
> Her arm around his neck
> Her foot upon his thigh
> His joy slipped inside
> Her rapture to engulf
> They have come together
> Their noses tip to tip.
>
> A pilgrim strolls around
> His drum wrapped in red cloth
> Black beard, long hair, bare feet
> In home-spun *Khadi* gown.
> Unwraps his village drum
> Softly begins to chant
> Fingers leap, rhythms beat
> Saris flash in the sun
> High pitch of ragas sung.

Facing south, the sun-god Surya rides his horse and the whole
edifice is mounted on great stone wheels to roll across the sky,
blazing with beauty, enlightenment for all. I unite my being with
this fabulous carving. For many years I had a recurring reverie of
a pilgrimage to Konarak with my love, seeing and feeling together
the finest human sculpture in the world. We delight in the

serpentine entwining of the snake-tails of the *naga* figures whose upper halves are human, occasionally playing a musical instrument or striking an amorous pose, lovers without legs, a land equivalent of mermaids.

Isfahan and Persepolis

From India to Iran, from Delhi to Isfahan, from 3 a.m. till dawn, our jet traversed an Islamic crescent path along a great circle route reversing the path that brought Islamic mosques to Hindu India; from a temple sculpture of representational frankness to the abstract witness of mosaics. In dawn sun-beams snow patches turned pink on the northern faces of mountains from Teheran to Isfahan, an interlude and prelude to our breakfast vista. In a small hotel we found a room whose balcony offered a striking view of the dome and minarets of the School of Theology. Imagine — breakfast in the sun, eye level to the mosaic tile floral dome, dominantly blue with yellow, white and green, one hundred yards away, an incredible perspective. We've learned to walk around a beautiful building with an eye out for some small hotel whose windows front on it. Sitting in the sun, feasting our eyes on these bright mosaic patterns, we sip our thick Turkish coffee, anticipating a new land, a new culture, the distinctive styles of Persian mosques.

What traveler hasn't felt the excitement of the first day in a new place. No matter how tired from the journey, a stroll to at least one mosque is imperative to collect some impressions before a long-awaited sleep. We approach the Shah Mosque by a long wide plaza whose rectangular reflecting pool doubles our view of the minarets and dome. Inside is another square reflecting pool with the same aesthetic effect, an Islamic motif that doubles all forms. We sit long beside the inner pool, allowing this new aesthetic to seep slowly into our consciousing, beginning to feel its unique powers. Gazing at the predominately blue dome I see the

whole sky brought down to earth in this mosque. And are not the
geometric patterns of green, white and gold, constellations of
stars glittering in the blue? Remove your sun glasses as you stroll
around the reflecting pool for they may screen out some
reflections. See the building in floating motion as you stroll. What
a marvelous invention was the arch and dome; no wonder the
name 'arch-itecture.' A great space could be enclosed for people
to meet, to celebrate, to worship.

By 4 p.m. we fell asleep, intending only a nap before supper
but the sandman drugged us until seven the next day. Our
morning begins at Jumma Mosque. In the anteroom to the main
dome I'm captivated by the panels of green vases full of mosaic
flowers as well as the raised tiles that simulate low-relief sculp-
ture. The flowers lend organic life to the abstract pattern, the
more striking for their rarity. We sit a long time watching the
morning light brighten different parts of the room. On the
northeast, east, is a small chapel-like room whose entrance-way is
a marvel, leading you into an interior with an altar flanked by two
high wooden step-chairs. The quality and variation in colors of
the mosaics strike me here. It seems as if the different shades
of blue in the sky are reproduced in this dome; the deep intense
blue of the zenith, the washed-out white-blue of the horizon, the
robin's egg blue of mid-sky.

Across the noontime we amble back to the main plaza through
streets full of wonderful smells. From one doorway the aroma of
baked bread, flat, three-eighths of an inch thick, eighteen inches
in diameter, warm from the adobe-dome oven. Lunch begins with
it. One vendor offers boiled corn-on-the-cob; another two-wheeled
cart contains a bubbling vat of large cooked beets. Navel oranges
provide dessert and we seat ourselves in front of the Lady Mosque
for two hours of reflection beside the pool. Lady Mosque has no
minarets, quite proper for its name, no phallus here, just the full
breast of the dome with the slight swell before it rounds to the
nipple on top. These two forms, minaret and dome, constitute the
architecture of the mosque whose decoration is the mosaic of
geometric design, occasional flowers, birds and butterflies.
Studying these patterns over several days, I feel their aesthetic to
consist of two elements: first, the straight line built into triangles,
squares, rectangles, hexagons, octagons and stars of many points,

combining, super-imposing, dividing space in endless angular variations. The second half of this artistic geometricism takes the curving line as basic, its primary mode branching into a reverse curve or coiling in upon itself and then changing direction to uncoil and coil again so as to fill all areas and corners of wall and dome and floor. I notice these simple patterns:

Added to the branching coil curves are floral blossoms, often placed at the center of the in-coil, whose petals become stars of four, six or eight points.

These decorative forms, I believe, emerge from the Islamic assimilation of the Greek geometric tradition combined with the Koran's prohibition against any naturalistic images of Allah, who is pure omnipotent transcendence. Islam's aesthetic solution to its theological vision finds perfect embodiment in the mosques of Isfahan. If you spend days in contemplation and perception here, you feel and see this theological conception. These mosaic patterns yield a marvelous precision, a rigorous determinism, abstractly depicted on these two natural forms of dome and minaret. Why are red and orange so little used in these mosaics? I find touches of red-brown in the blossoms across the top of the east facade of Shah Mosque and a little in the vertical panels. So the Isfahan palette is a background of blue with yellow and green, black and white.

Anticipating a clear sunset and near full moon, we are glad to create our own supper free from a restaurant. Nothing simpler. We step into a delicatessen, purchase breaded veal chops, a mixture of carrots and cauliflower in vinegar, a fist-size ball of split peas mixed with unknown spices, a bottle of milk, a pint of yogurt, potato salad and for dessert, dried sweet cherries. Moving a small table from our room onto the balcony, we spread our feast while the setting sun is reflected off the dome of the School of Theology, pinking the white, and the near full moon turns from a daytime white to a nighttime yellow, softening all it touches. Here is our banquet, beautiful and simple, laid in a splendid setting, impromptu and convenient. As the chill of evening descends we dispose of some paper wrappers, slip into bed under three blankets and sleep till sunrise, waking for a new day at the mosques. We dress quickly to arrive at the Shah Mosque when it opens at eight to contemplate the only half hour of sun on the southwest facade. The low slanting sunbeams also penetrate deep into the dome room, bringing even greater brilliance to the mosaic colors.

Tap, tap — tap, tap, tap — the hammers fly, resting only to focus on the design in the hammered metal work — trays, plates, cups, coffee pots. Who can pass by these little shops along the streets beside the mosques? Step in and watch. Aren't they doing in miniature what the mosques before them show — minute abstract designs in fine hammered arabesques like the mosaics on the domes? As a child I watched my father hammer metal as a hobby, copper and aluminum, so this rhythmic tapping was childhood music in my ears. I feel at home in this distant land. How lovely is the harmony between craft and architecture. Allah's omnipotence knows no bounds.

How one first leans of a distant place may well create the mood in which you visit it. Take Shiraz, Iran, for instance. Long ago reading Thoreau's *A Week On the Concord and Merrimack Rivers,* I came upon the Persian poet Sadi, author of the *Gulistan,* whose home, Gail now reminds me, was in Shiraz. So this city is at once invested with personal meaning — that wisdom Thoreau learns from Sadi. A small memorial park creates the mood of Sadi's rose garden while we stroll among the fragrant flower beds. Pure relaxation settles over us as we recall Thoreau's extract from the *Gulistan*:

> *A good and pious man reclined his head on the*
> *bosom of contemplation, and was absorbed in the*

The metaphor of a garden: a place of quiet, peace, meditation — fragrance, blossoms, paths — pleasure, happiness, bliss. The Gulistan, the Garden of Eden, the Zen Garden. We make gardens to nurture our reveries, to transform our being, to liberate our self. In a person's garden you can find the contours of their religion. I found no snake or fruit in Japanese Zen gardens. I might travel around the world again in a study of the religion of gardens. Do you grow vegetables or flowers? Are there fountains or ponds?

Spring has come to Shiraz, the whole city is a garden, streets divided by a median of flower beds, Sadi's roses everywhere. What better ideal for the design of a city — to be a garden. On the bus riding from Shiraz to Persepolis we see a New Mexico landscape, and where orchards are irrigated, peach and apple trees blossom. In villages familiar mud-adobe walls blend with the earth. No building material seems better suited to remind us of our relationship to the land. Treeless mountain ridges of reddish sandstone border the valley of Persepolis, one of those great sacred places of the world. Sacred to fire, eternal fire, symbol of the highest for Zoroastrians, monument to ancient Persian glory built by Darius, Xerxes, Artaxerxes, destroyed and burned by Alexander, but still magnificent. Stone doesn't burn.

Here the stairway achieves unique embodiment, leading to or away from gates of power. In the low-relief carving on the sides of the stairways, monotonous on first glance, but infinitely and subtly various on closer attention, a stately gracefulness complements the massive power of the gates. Gertrude Stein would admire this variation in repetition. Bearers of tribute from many peoples and many lands, from India and Africa, come to Persepolis, all carved in their own style of dress, their faces modeled in distinctive ethnic features. We note varying modes of transport and characteristic kinds of gifts. History parades before our eyes. To see this low relief with a maximum of aesthetic joy you have to calculate when the sun will be at forty-five degrees to the plane of the surface in order to produce the shadows that will etch each figure into clear portrait. Light is everything to low relief. Moreover, light is of the essence of the semi-desert lands of the Middle East and the Southwest of the United States: clarity and brilliance astound the eyes, dazzling from the domes of mosques, sharpening shadows of Persepolis columns and gates, flooding the plazas of our Southwest Indian pueblos. A traveler at Persepolis needs several days at least to make a log of places and sun-positions. Then take your seat and view the stately homage.

> Legions of Medes and Persians march
> In low relief on Persepolis walls
> Best seen by shadow etching bands
> From sun at forty-five degrees.
>
> Darius and Xerxes built Colossi here
> To magnify their power and grace,
> Homage to the everlasting Fire
> Sacred image of the eternal One.
>
> Processions of the nations tribute bear
> Beneath graceful stairways of low wide tread.
> Above even the Kings a phoenix flies
> Ever reborn from its own fire ashes.

Part way up the hillside behind Persepolis, carved into the rock, are the tombs of Artaxerxes II and III. From here a sweeping view of the landscape of ruins spreads below. You can only wonder how it once appeared, for no architecture remains today similar to this expanse of stairways, gates and flat-roofed temples. No early traveler's description or sketch survives from its living years. What can restoration really achieve here? I talk with Italian masons who have been working for two years moving massive blocks back into position on some gates. The results will not give the sense of the temple. The loss is permanent; our low-relief panels, though glorious to see, belong to a fractured aesthetic.

Seated in the grand tomb entrance, eyes drifting over the plain, I slip into a reverie on the meaning of stone tombs. Why is this craving to be remembered so strong, this urge to mark the

earth with a personal symbol? What is the cost in human lives and labor, the misery of masses, so that a king's name is known? Today I know the names of Darius and Xerxes but what does it matter? What does it mean? Suppose there were no Persepolis, would the life of the spirit be any different? Our sense of incompleteness makes us vain. Such vanity is not present in a complete person liberated from desires. Tombs mark a failure in the persons so immortalized. Perhaps this is the meaning of that strange monolithic figure on one gateway — a man-phoenix whose wings tell us of the flight of the spirit from such earth-bound vanity.

On a rainy day another world awaits your exploration in the covered bazaar of Shiraz. Everyone can find something here to bargain for. My fancy is captivated by the Persian rugs, thousands in a hundred shops, seemingly endless, the colors and designs so enticing as to make a choice of one impossible. As I study the intricate designs woven in the rugs I see the same geometric aesthetic that characterizes the mosaic patterns of the mosques and the hammered metal work. This identity of pattern clearly demonstrates the pervasive character of a culture's aesthetic vision. With this insight I begin to look afresh at the designs in the hammered metal work. Yes, here too the same impulse is manifest. When you stroll through this bazaar, leave time for tea or Turkish coffee in several of the more beautiful interiors, converse, admire, garner experience for a wider taste.

Another day, returning from Persepolis to Shiraz, strolling from the bus station to our restaurant, how lovely to encounter hawkers selling spring daffodils in the street, and at our table pussy willows dust yellow pollen on our tablecloth. I reflect on the universal meaning of flowers, symbols of affection and peace, of loveliness and passion, grown to delight the eye and nose. It is possible, I know, to speak by means of flowers.

In the mosaics of the Pars Museum, formerly a private home, flowers and birds are inlaid in exquisite grace. Here the shades of red and orange missing in Isfahan glow in balanced compositions. This house and garden are a gulistan where I feel I could settle my spirit for a long rest. I wonder what it might be like to live for years in this city of Shiraz. Our days here have added to the mosaic of our lives, inlaid fragments of beauty beyond our expectations.

Greek Temples

We sleep quietly in our small VW station wagon perched on a cliff above the sea, on the ancient Roman Road, *Antica Via Flacca*, north of Gaeta, waves lapping on the rocks one hundred feet below. The ancient stone embankments laid so masterfully to weather centuries prepare us for Greek temples built by colonists long before the Roman Road. We live on roads now: traveling, sleeping, eating, writing, reading in or near our VW, driven over the Alps south through Italian towns and cities, from winter to early spring, from snowbound passes to fields of blossoms. Often we camp beside temple ruins, feeling and comparing these pre-Christian European temples with Iran, India, Java and Japan.

A new mode of travel has its own style and rhythm. Our back-packs are put away, no more buses, trains, ships or planes. Every night we enjoy the same bed, our foam-rubber pad unrolled in the station wagon. Food and clothes are stowed under the hood. Our simple meals require no cooking — salads, eggnogs, bread and cheese, fruit and wine. It was possible to free camp in beautiful places and rarely were we asked to move on. Keep an eye alert for junk that will just suit your needs. We found rubber car mats, plastic pitchers, folding chair, folding table, sponges, broom, dust pan, stories to tell along the way. Five months of saved hotel bills purchased our VW-home. This style of living we developed in the United States and Mexico with years of practice. To find your private camping place, take a road off a road off the road you're driving on, from pavement to gravel to dirt track or grassy lane. Ask the farmer, the shepherd, the rancher, the peasant if you see them; their hospitality is gracious. We are often given vegetables or fruits in season.

On the way to Paestum we stop at the eighth century B.C. ruin at Cunae and explore the carved rooms of the extensive cave in which the Sibyl gave out oracular truths. According to legend Aeneas consulted this oracle before his descent into Hades. A pentagonal hallway with branching corridors and a central room cut into a sandstone ridge demonstrate an architectural form like the cave-temples of India. The acropolis shows only a floor plan, an oracular warning of what we will experience at many temple sites. But Paestum is a grand exception, three standing temples have all their columns and lintels in place. As everywhere the roofs and relief-carving from the entablature are gone. For these we visit museums, an aesthetic discontinuity. Here the Greek temple aesthetic of harmoniously proportioned rectangles, horizontal and vertical, supported by columns, sinks into my consciousing. Without the arch, Greek architecture was severely limited in the span of open space it could create within a temple not interrupted by support columns. For me the best vantage point for viewing a Greek temple is forty-five degrees out from a corner from where I can see both side and end, columns and corridors, entablature and frieze. In a sense Greek temples might be said to be cubistic in architectural forms, or ''rectangularistic.'' I feel this stylistic power in them. Indian and Egyptian architecture also lacked the arch but some inner impulse drove them to pile block on block, skyward, creating *gopuram*-tower or pyramid. Not so the Greek for whom a low pitched roof seemed sufficient to their spirit, perhaps for gods who dwelled on the earth, terrestrial rather than celestial.

Among several strategies for finding free camping places on a coast road is one that often yields a spectacular vista. Keep an eye peeled for headlands where the old road went out around the tip while the new road tunnels through the rock. At either end of the tunnel you may find a track connecting the old road; follow it, and with good luck you'll find a perch on the tip of the headland cliff, out of sight of the new road, from where your view sweeps over bays and points, rugged hillsides strewn with a yellow flowering bush or terraced olive slopes, a fishing village of red-tiled roofs snug in a cove. The sea shows many colors from light turquoise blue to dark purple, from sandy brown to sparkling foam.

Sicily, an ancient Greek colony, lures us. Our anticipation is heightened by the story Vincent Cronin tells in *The Golden Honeycomb*, our book for reading aloud down this Italian-Calabrian coast. From a high promontory above the town of Palmi we see our ferry crossing the straits of Messina. After the night's rain white and pink pear and apricot blossoms shimmer. Below, a muddy river spews brown water from recent rains into the blue Mediterranean, forming a great hemispherical cap in front of the river mouth. As the tide ebbs, the brown water is drawn along the coast until it meets dark blue-purple currents that prob it. We have a grand view of the coast of Sicily. I like to see a new land thus, spreading away before me.

On Sicily we go at once to Naxos, the oldest known Greek settlement, their beginning, our beginning. Its massive stone blocks convey an ancient presence of solidity, endurance, order, balance. Some strange power awes me. I walk the wall in silent meditation but have no aesthetic pleasure here. It is too ruinous. No portions of buildings or sculpture remain. Strange, how a presence of spirit still remains. What kind of feeling is this?

From afar Greek sailors navigated by the smoking top of Mt. Etna. All day we drive around the shore of the *golfo di Catania*, viewing Etna from many perspectives. Across the *golfo* from Etna and the city of Catania we camp on a spit of land east of the village of Brucoli. From here the perfect symmetry of the mountain shows two sloping upward curves, the top half white with snow. Immediately across the small cove the rising sun strikes the facade of the town church illuminating the same upward sloping curves, a lovely conjunction. The sun reflected in the windows of the village houses sets them shimmering like a hundred mirrors, dazzling spots of a musical score. Unexpectedly the church bells toll the host. We remain here several days focused on Etna and the church. In my reveries I imagine Plato's visits to Syracuse to educate the tyrant Dionysius. I recall Archimedes' discovery of the principle of specific gravities while in the bath. This landscape was their landscape.

North of *Siracusa* we wander among the ruins of Megera Hyblea, a place of the dead, a necropolis of tombs, perhaps fifty rectangular boxes, each side a great slab of stone, carefully smoothed and fitted, small and large, for children and adults.

What belief demands such careful preservation of the dead? This ruin now stands in the midst of an oil refinery belching polluting gases. Archimedes would be excited to see such technical ingenuity, a tradition he began. Plato would have some doubts; mechanical power is not wisdom.

Imagine the pleasure of making an outdoor theatre whose seats, aisles, steps and stage are cut from a hillside of solid stone commanding a splendid view across the city and harbor of Syracuse. In one-third of a hollow hemisphere the rows of seats and backs are shaped to fit your body curves. A cool spring gushes forth out of the rock behind the top row. Monolithic architecture has a special charm and technique, cut from the top down, rather than built up of blocks. Which seats did Plato and Archimedes occupy? I sit in many places seeking their perspectives. Envision some triremes at anchor in the harbor bound for Athens tomorrow.

Our pilgrimage in Sicily seeks out Greek ruins, not knowing before we arrive what remains to be seen. Guidebooks we have come to distrust so we explore any site marked on our map, often disappointed as today at Camarina, Gela, Eraclea Minoa. All too ruinous, and I wish for the carved detail of Indian temples. Nevertheless, at the small museum of Gela I begin to appreciate the delightful humor in the scenes painted on Greek vases. How often Pan enlivens the frolic with his curved erect cock and his slightly leering smile. Beware of Pan. The vases give me Greek life and style, banquets, hunting scenes, love-making, worship, boats, chariots, clothing and hair styles — the naturalism and humanism of Greek religion. Another day we take our lunch on the large monolithic blocks of stone at Selinunte. Before the reconstructed temple I feel starkness and massiveness. Who moved these gigantic blocks? What titans dwelt here?

A titan of modern drama was born in Agrigento, Luigi Pirandello, that most philosophical of dramatists. His boyhood home overlooks the sea. Surely he drew upon some ancient Greek spirit in the ruined outdoor theatre, fumes of Aristophanes mixed with Sophocles. I first read his plays twenty-five years ago yet his wit and epistemology are with me still. He, too, may have strolled among these Greek temples on the acropolis dazzling in the afternoon sunlight. From this height I search the valley below for a possible camping place from which the whole acropolis will be in view. Why not beside that small ruin in the grove? Later we park in the almond grove beside the tomb of Theron, once tyrant of this city. Our eyes sweep the whole acropolis, three temples, Concordia in the middle, the afternoon sun turning the stone a golden-brown, the meadow bedecked with blossoms, yellow daisies, orange-red poppies and purple thistle. We dine and sleep here, eyes magnetically drawn again and again to the acropolis of temples. My dominant feeling of the Greek aesthetic in these temples at Agrigento is starkness and abstractness. The paint and relief sculpture is gone; balance, proportion and ratio form an architectural geometry, a visual Euclid. Without the relief sculpture we don't feel inclined to linger for days at a temple as we did in India. This missing feature much alters our response.

Strange, how one comes home. The temple at Segesta on its lonely perch in the mountains of western Sicily I had looked at many times in a painting by my father that hung in his library. But I did not know then it was Segesta. Usually Greek colonies were on the coast. Why did they come to this interior mountainous region? This I wonder in my meditation as I sit in their ancient theatre high on a hillside overlooking this rugged land. Descending the hill from the theatre we spy a perfect perspective of the temple, at eye level a quarter of a mile across the valley if we can park near a sheep corral. Friendly shepherds welcome us, one speaking English, learned in Scotland as a prisoner of war in World War II. Our angle of vision is forty-five degrees to the corner of the temple, caught next morning in the sunlight as we lie on our foam mattress in the VW, the rear door raised. What a vision to open my eyes on day after day.

At different times each day we stroll across to the temple to see and feel the various textures wrought by sunlight on stone. Its interior walls and roof are missing, allowing the sunlight to illumine.and shadow the complete ring of columns and entablature. The brown-yellow sandstone blocks turn golden at sunrise and sunset. Some days I take my book or journal to read or write, seated in or beside this lovely edifice.

On the slopes of the hill behind the theatre we renew an old pastime, hunting for potsherds, pieces of Greek pottery, and find the terrain littered with jug and cup handles, rims, bottoms, sides of pots. But even more exciting we find many cisterns shaped like beehives, the narrow top entrance covered by large stone slabs so the sheep won't fall in. I want to lower myself in one but lack any equipment. How many homes were scattered across these slopes? Finding cisterns all around generates a powerful sense of the vitality of this hillside. It comes alive for us.

Each morning and evening the shepherds give us fresh warm ricotta cheese. Invited into their hut in the evening, we watch them making it. Into a large caldron, three feet high, Angelo pours sheep-milk and water, about half and half, to which he adds a fistful of salt. He stirs it occasionally until it just comes to a boil and thickens. Two men can barely lift it off the fire. With a wooden dipper he deftly ladles the coagulated brew into woven baskets of two- and three-quart measure. The liquid drains through the basket weave, leaving the solid mass to set. The drained liquid is caught in a pail and poured back into more milk to make the next batch. Our feast is a dipper of warm cheese in a copper bowl, eaten with a soup spoon, with a unique flavor that I cannot describe, a delicacy to be known only at the precise time when the cheese is taken off the fire, a precious experience for us, our own special meaning for Segesta.

Last evening I watched the horse tethered near our car enjoy a strange meal. He ate prickly thistle, especially liking the blue blossoms but devouring prickly leaves and stalks. How cautiously and delicately he bit off the leaves, not closing his lips tight, rolling them gently back into the rear of his mouth where, I think, they were combined with a large cud into which the prickles would be absorbed and bent, perhaps softened by his saliva. Exactly how he managed this feat I don't know, but that he enjoyed it immensely was clearly visible, a feast I was not inclined to imitate.

Time to soak up the essence of a place we find crucial in our traveling. Today we sit in the Greek theatre for the morning, high up on the slope, writing, reading, gazing into the surrounding valley. To slow the pace of time seems to give me space for meditations that bridge present and distant past. I sit with ancient Greeks waiting for a performance to begin. At every Greek site we find a theatre testifying to their widespread love of dramatic art, a part of their religious practice, I think. In the evening I go to sleep gazing at Segesta in the moonlight. The stone lacks polish to glisten in the moon, but the shadows of the columns hold a blue-gray mystery. When I awake at dawn my eyes open on the sunlit temple.

Legend has it that Daedalus came to the oracle at Erice to offer the famous carved honeycomb now lost to art. Pitched thousands of feet above the sea, the town shows no remains of the oracle now, but the place was invested with meaning for us from our reading of Vincent Cronin's *The Golden Honeycomb*. Here was the temple sacred to the goddess of love that once stood on a separate pinnacle where stands today the ruin of a Norman castle. Legend tells us the temple was a sanctuary for women, managed by a priestess of oracular powers, and that a pilgrimage to it might yield love, solace and protection. Shrouded in mist, the streets are wonderfully silent; silence hangs over the town. In the end, perhaps love has nothing to say, it can only be felt. We drive down the narrow winding road with this feeling between us.

Other civilizations besides the Greek have left their mark on Sicily. Roman villas and Norman churches contrast with Greek temples. In Montreale we visit the Norman Church of King William the Good. Its marvelous interior of mosaics and marble — not painting, not low-relief, not tapestry — captures the mood of its Old and New Testament subjects, saints and sinners. In the apse looking down on everyone is the large portrait of Christ, his face radiant with human understanding. His expression beckons so strongly I return on the next several days with deepening friendship. No other Christ has so transfixed me. In the adjacent cloister I stroll between the double row of columns. Each column has a distinctive capital and a different mosaic pattern. In Palermo similar mosaics excite us at the Cappella Palatina and the Church of Martorana. At the last an Easter service is in progress, chanted and sung by sonorous voices, the sun streaming down in spots on the singers, my ears and eyes filled with joy, the mosaics shining, the music rising, a glorious event.

We return to Greek ruins, visiting Solunto, an imposing site on a hillside overlooking the sea. Some floor mosaics are still in place, progenitor of the Norman mosaics. Next to the theatre is a large bathing pool, streets are clearly distinguishable, and the home at the end of the main street on the edge of the sea cliff enjoys an unrivalled panorama. Cisterns are full of water and the drainage system is still working after 2500 years. No autos, no smog; beautiful stone houses, mosaic floors, theatre and pool, water and food, wine and philosophy — what else could one desire?

Ten kilometers west of Cefalu we camp in the lee of a ruined castle on the coast to break the buffeting sea wind. Our style of free camping often attracts a curious and friendly shepherd or farmer interested in how we fix our bed in the rear of the VW station wagon and cook our supper in one pot. On this evening he returns bearing a gift of large tree-ripened lemons for our larder, lemons that last us over a week in lunchtime lemonade. How typical such giving is by rural people wherever we travel.

Who hasn't looked at a map of Italy and wanted to drive along the coast of its heel and toe following the shore curves and waves. On an open bluff overlooking the gulf of Taranto I watch the sun melt into the sea. The water glows pink and golden. During the night I hear village bells strike the hours. Before dawn I awaken to see the waning quarter moon and morning star rise. Slowly bands of shell-pink color the horizon. The thin red arc of sun grows into a glowing red ball in the mist. My reveries are of a life roaming free in pursuit of the aesthetic in nature and culture, from one beautiful place to another, meditating, reading and writing.

> A spotlight of sunshine
> Racing across the hillside
> Dark purple shadows
> Scatter on the sea.
> Newborn leaves
> Sun-yellow-green
> Checker the slopes
> Skimmed by swallows.
> Pear blossom white
> Pink apricot blooms
> Wild thistle blue
> My love I long for you.

If you land in Greece by ship at Igoumenitsa, commence your journey with a consultation of the ancient oracle at Dodoni, near the city of Ioannina. Sit in the ancient theatre and meditate on the oracle's reply while the beauty of the place seeps into you. Sit still and listen. You too are an oracle through which the world speaks.

Waiting, lingering, we wonder how this oracle came to be located in this long narrow valley, bursting with springtime, bordered by snow-capped mountain ridges. Human beings are often sensitive to the aesthetic setting of sacred precincts. How exactly does each aid the other? To experience this conjunction, a whispering within us murmurs ''wander as you are.''

Reading aloud *The World of Odysseus* by M. T. Finley, we feel Ithaca beckoning. The names on our map of the Peloponnesus come alive; Nestor's Palace near Pilos lures us. On our way through stringtime air that vibrates with bird songs, we wander among the blocks of stone of the temple ruins at Stratos, guided by a small girl who gathers a bouquet gift of wild blossoms. Winding around sharp hairpin turns on a bumpy gravel road we spot a small folding table that must have fallen from a truck. Gail jokes that around the next turn we'll find a folding chair. We do. The gods provide for our needs.

A few evenings later we reach the ruins of Illis, a wide pastoral valley dappled with daisy and clover blossoms, peaceful to the fluctuations of human moods. Seated on a large block of stone in a meadow, I wonder that this is all that remains of proud Illis, of the ancient school of philosophy founded by Phaedo. A wave of tiredness sweeps over me, twelve months among temples in many lands. We must look for a resting place, our awareness is saturated.

For many European tourists Olympus is a high point of their journey. For me it is an aesthetic low point, too ruinous, piles of fragments, not a building standing. I compare it to temples in India where we stayed for days enchanted by the sculpture and architecture. I become deeply aware of the contrast between Greek ruins and Indian temples and wonder how people become ecstatic over these fragments. Imagination creates an aura in these ruins. A cultural provincialism and a linear view of history unduly magnify this Greek heritage. I am moved only by Praxiteles' ''Hermes'' in the museum. Before it I sit for long periods. A masterpiece one knows at once without doubt, as Gertrude Stein wrote in *What are Masterpieces?* No comparisons are in order. The restorations in the museum of the east and west pediments of the Temple of Zeus show ingenious compositions within the elongated geometrical shape of a pediment that cramps the figures.

On the way to Bassae (Vasse) from Olympus, we notice an archeological sign in Greek for ancient Skilloundia pointing to a dirt road winging up into the hills. Tempted on, we park the car and climb the hilltop where we find floor-blocks of a small temple. The meadow below offers an ideal camping place. A farm boy returning with his pail of fresh goat-milk watches me beating eggs with a spoon for our omelette supper and uninhibited, hands me a fork, to better do my work. I liked that. His knowledge of world geography surprised us; a bright lad.

The temple of Bassae stands on a high mountain ridge in a wild countryside. Why was it built there? The architect of Bassae, Ictinus, also designed the Parthenon of Athens. His work at Bassae still stands, a small temple, columns and walls in place with a measured harmony of proportions. In the main hall are half-columns cut from blocks projecting from the wall, an unusual motif.

As I sit contemplating this temple I hear the braying of a donkey with its wonderful pathetic voice, a sound I like, yet it might be judged one of the most unmusical voices in the animal kingdom. But the donkey does not hush for that. He brays with gusto low and clear over hill and valley — 'heehaw, heehaw, heehaw' — breathing in and out it seems. Temples crumble while he brays on.

A ruin that is too ruinous may come alive if you are reading about the lives and events that transpired there. Nestor's Palace at Pilos came alive through Finley's *World of Odysseus*, and we could fancy Telemachus' ships sailing into the bay, a young man come for an old man's wisdom many centuries ago, the oldest place in time we have reached on this journey. How does our consciousing transform the dead crumbled present into a living present effortlessly bridging centuries of time? Seated in the Queen's bath I ruminate on this.

A small lad who learned English in Toronto, Canada showed us the track to an isolated beach on the shore of the southern Peloponnese near the village of Finikous. This lovely place faces a bay sheltered by two islands whose lighthouses blink at me through the night. On seeing it we know at once this is one of our special places, a dream come true, a place to rest. We discard our clothes and swim. This Mediterranean Sea fulfills all romantic dreams. Out of the water we rig up our fly for shade beside the VW, fix our favorite salad lunch. Here we can bathe, read, swim, write, love, sleep and sun undisturbed, that periodic recuperation essential to a traveler. The afternoon slips away as I gaze unfocused on the glistening waves, hearing their lapping on the beach.

In the fourth century B.C., Plato founded an Academy in Athens, one branch of which, years later, moved to Constantinople with the Eastern Roman Empire and when the Turks captured Byzantine, returned to Mistras, near Sparta. Its last teacher was Giorgius Gemistos Plethon, who lived in Mistras from 1393 to 1442, two thousand years after Plato, and gave the Platonic torch to Italian Humanists. The small Byzantine churches of Mistras, whose interior frescoes and exterior brick and stone manifest a meditative, sometimes even a brooding mood, evoke from me a long period of zazen seated in the Nunnery where Gail lit a candle for Ogata-san. I am carried back to Kyoto, to morning meditations in the *zendo* of Chotoku-in Temple before breakfast with Ogata. He, too, was a subtle teacher. Seated on a bench on the west side of the Ayia Sophia, a Mistras gem, I listen to Gail reading aloud from Plato's *Republic* and wonder if Gemistos Plethon sat here with *The Republic* in hand. I recall my first reading of *The Republic* at age seventeen, a gift of a visiting friend; how deeply I believed in the Ideal of the Good and the rational ordering of my life. From that time onward I have loved, enjoyed and lived in the pursuit of philosophy. The domes and towers, arched windows and doorways of Mistras absorb me not only architecturally but evoke this reverie across several days on Plato's Academy and my life as a teacher. I endow Mistras with my individual meaning, another art the traveler can employ to enrich experience.

On a grassy hillside high above Lerni I look down across the bay to Naplion, intrigued by the shape of the bay weaving in amongst the curving shores, lacing in the islands, more blue than the sky. I awake at five with the earliest pre-dawn light while the stars still shine, and lie watching them fade as the horizon becomes purple, then pink-orange till the bright sun just winks over the bare mountain ridge behind Naplion. For the last several days we have encountered flocks of sheep blocking the road, freshly sheared on their way to summer pastures. How clean and trim they look, light and frisky, a little embarrassed by their scanty dress, bells ringing gaily. In one village the small plaza was heaped with piles of shorn wool.

Eleven years ago I felt the excitement of Mycenae, Homeric legends brought to life. Today, after India and Iran, I see insignificant ruins. Even the Lion Gate cannot touch the stairways of Persepolis. I feel it is a tourist attraction living on the worship of classical civilization fostered by a myopic view of the past. What of the art and history of other civilizations? The textbooks' ravings over these stone lions seem the ravings of mad men. They simply do not compare aesthetically with the sculpture of India. Tracing our cultural heritage to the history of Mycenae blinds us to its lack of artistic quality.

> Tourism is a click
> A million cameras blink
> A tour bus horn bleats
> Another ride beneath a blazing sun
> Till the next click
> Click, click, click, click
> Human vision disappears.

The theatre at Epidaurus remains magnificent. To sit there, to be in the audience, to see the chorus enter and hear their chant, to witness the treachery, murder, passion and misery, the flowering of consciousness, the distinctive human virtues: a performance by the Greek National Theatre moves one deeply. If the human psyche is fractured, ancient Greek psychiatrists knew a shock treatment combining noise and smoke, snakes and screams, steam and sweat, darkness and terror, followed by gentle art therapy and creative freedom. In his *Colossus of Maroussi* Henry Miller sings a beautiful paean to Epidaurus: he found it to be "the great peace, the peace of the heart, which comes with surrender." Seated on the stone benches 2500 years old, I wonder about the lives of each person who has also sat there across so many years; what collective wisdom we would share.

Everyone goes to Athens, to the Acropolis, to the Parthenon: crowds with little interest or knowledge, tourists following their guides like innocent sheep bleating inanities to each other about hotels, food and home, hardly looking at what is pointed to. It becomes increasingly difficult to really see, to contemplate, the beauty of such places, to sit a while ruminating, meditating, reflecting, open to the ghosts of Pericles and Socrates. We learn to come early before the tour buses arrive and stay late after they've left. In these quiet periods gazing on the Parthenon I gather together the many ways in which architectural forms and sculptural relief express distinctive human ambiances. I begin to grasp the beliefs and values of diverse cultures expressed in their portrayals of living things, persons and deities. I am struck by the ever-resurgent novelty of human activity.

Our living among Greek temples in Sicily and Greece came to an end, appropriately, with a journey to Delphi in hopes that the oracle might give us a message, but we suffered a Socratic fate in that it spoke only in the negative, ''Tourism annihilates creative travel.'' In Athens I purchased Karl Jasper's two volumes of *The Great Philosophers,* launched into fresh reading with all the joy I find in the furnace of philosophy, a new intellectual journey. Was this an answer to the oracle? Is not the journey of our spirit exactly what Socrates discovered? Tourism is merely the body traveling in space but my voyage of the spirit gathers together the personal meaning of temple places for reflective pondering. Isn't this the Delphic wisdom I can learn?

About the Author

Paul F. Schmidt teaches philosophy at the University of New Mexico and enjoys a rhythm that allows alternate academic years on leave for writing and travel. His interest in the interactions of literature and philosophy began in Honors Seminars in both fields at the University of Rochester where he received his A.B. in 1947. After completing his Ph.D. in Philosophy, Yale University in 1951, he taught at Oberlin College until 1965. Recent alternate years have included writing and travel from Newfoundland to Mayan Central America, from Switzerland to his beloved Bahia Kino on the Gulf of California.

Temple Reflections is set in Century Textbook — the text 10 on 13, the poems 10 on 11; chapter titles are 20 point Century Textbook Italic. The text paper is Hammermill Opaque, 60 lb. It was typeset by Carolynne Colby and printed by the Valliant Company, Albuquerque, New Mexico. Sally Schuh made the drawings from the author's sketches. The photo on page 80 is by Edward Kohnstamm.

Hummingbird Press was founded in 1970 to publish original works in literature and philosophy. Its name is borrowed from a spring along the trail to Mogollon Baldy in New Mexico's Gila Wilderness. The hummingbird, a female *Loddigesia*, on the title page, was drawn by Phyllis Cohen.